# LIGHT AND IMAGES

ADRIENNE VON SPEYR

# Light and Images

## Elements of Contemplation

Translated by David Schindler, Jr.

IGNATIUS PRESS    SAN FRANCISCO

Original German edition:
*Das Licht und die Bilder: Elemente der Kontemplation*
© 1955, Johannes Verlag, Einsiedeln, Switzerland
Second edition © 1986

Cover art:
*The Ascension of Christ*

Fra Angelico
Galleria Nazionale d'Arte Antica, Rome, Italy
© Scala/Art Resource, New York

Cover design by Roxanne Mei Lum

© 2004 by Ignatius Press, San Francisco
All rights reserved
ISBN 0−89870−883−4
Library of Congress Control Number 2004103524
Printed in the United States of America ∞

# Contents

God's infinite life and vision is opened to man. Man and world are ontologically ordered to the Son and must be interpreted accordingly. The center of the world: the Cross, wherein God's entire love, and man's entire disobedience and entire obedience, is revealed. Contemplation must be catholic: both universal and personal. Its community-building function.

The loss of a sense for God and for his will because of sin. The Son, as man, re-establishes this sense. The Our Father as inserting the believer into obedience to God. Active love as knowing God and God's will. The incorporation of those who love into the objective love of the Church and the Son.

The grace of faith as the most living life and at the same time as that which comprehends all of life's movement. Faith as light, which envelopes everything that is illuminated. Light as gift and as appropriated responsibility. Christ as light and as illuminated by faith. Light as the "with", as participation. Integration of one's entire everyday life into light.

The Yes without shadows; every Yes stems from prayer. The sinner's being carried in prayer through others' powers of love, so that he can be freed from the shadows of his sin. The shadows that are eliminated, those that remain, and those that are newly formed. The Cross overshadows prayer. Anonymity and the inseparability of the good from the bad shadows. Discrepancy between the fulfilled meaning of the words of prayer and their emptiness and void. Reservations in "suffering-with", and their being overcome in love.

The night of creation, of sin, and of the Cross: their interpenetration. The Lord distributes his night, but it remains something suffered in him. It is present as a mystery in every faith, and therefore concerns everyone. Analogy between the night of the Cross and Christian existence. The prayer of the day in relation to the night. The prayer of the night made out of the night: out of the Lord's night and into the night of the Church and of faith. The necessity of hearing the cry of abandonment. Dying to one's own life in the contemplation of the Cross in order to live on through love.

6. Awakening from the Night . . . . . . . . 77

7. Drawing Near . . . . . . . . . . . . . . . 91

Word. The power of God's Word in heaven. Contemplation as responding to the Word; inclusion and distance. The unity of being and act in the Son, the unity of contemplation and action in the one contemplating.

For us, the world consists of images, and these must be interpreted in view of the Son. The uniqueness of all images of the world; their value for God. Jesus' image of the world is open and accessible to the believer. Distance and proximity to things in faith. God-willed joy in the world, but a joy ordered to Christ. The beauty of things, Christian art. The eternal dimension of images, their relationship with God's Word. Images in the sphere and on the margins of contemplation. Prayer and constant everyday interchange of image and frame.

The Son as image of the Father. The concreteness of heaven in revelation. The images of the apocalypse; the same eyes of the visionary see both heaven and earth. "Today you will be with me in paradise"; "I see heaven opened up": the image-transcending presence of heaven. The transference of earthly reality into the kingdom of heaven. Objectivity as the precondition for such a transposition: both in the Incarnation (heaven coming to earth) and for the eschatological promise (earth entering into heaven). Preserving on earth the images of heaven. Contemplation of heaven possible only within the concreteness of revelation. Earthly and heavenly contemplation complement one another. Christ, as the God-man, is the measure for faith's contemplation.

The uncloseable gap in the contemplation of the Lord's miracle and his essence as God made man. In the parables, there is at first a continuity between the earthly and the divine, but then the chasm appears. The parables are simple and yet contain an inexhaustible mystery. The Son's capacity to create images of the kingdom of heaven and to fill them with eternal life.

The world that can be divided up numerically as the revelation of the one God. Man, woman, and child as image. The holy family as a higher image. Jesus' human nature as the manifestation of the entire triune life of God. Number and number series as an image. The entire economy of salvation as rooted in the trinitarian God. The Our Father and the images that the Son places in it. Man as image. The Son in his fulness as the recapitulation and unity of the world, as the comprehensive image.

# Introduction

There is no end to teaching about prayer, especially contemplative prayer. Adrienne von Speyr has already published an extensive work on the subject, *The World of Prayer*,[1] in which she descends from the eternal conversation within God himself, passes through the prayer of Christ and Mary, and leads us to the fullness of the states of life and situations within the Church: the prayer of those who are consecrated to God, of those with the office of priesthood, of the married laity who live in the world; the prayer of people at different ages and stages in life.

The present little book complements the more extensive work in a decisive way. Here, the theme is the highest and broadest theological presuppositions of contemplative prayer. The whole is governed, just as it is in Thomas Aquinas, by the reciprocal relationship between "light" (*lumen*) and "image" (*species*).

God's revelation is twofold: on the one hand, the communication of his eternal *light* of truth, of life,

---

[1] Adrienne von Speyr, *The World of Prayer*, trans. Graham Harrison (San Francisco: Ignatius Press, 1985).

and of love, which becomes visible and manifest to us in Jesus Christ ("I am the light of the world") and sinks into our heart as the light of the Holy Spirit ("*O lux beatissima*"), of faith, of hope and of love, so that the light is both present before us [*gegenständlich*] and present within us [*in-ständlich*], both objective and subjective. As such, it therefore binds us to and gives us a share in the object of God's revelation in the most intimate way possible. This light of divine truth and love that pours itself out into the world also appears, however, in the form of the "shadows" and the "night" of the Cross, at least insofar as the Cross is the Redeemer's atoning and reconciling assumption of human vanity and darkness, a work that places the contemplating believer also under this same law.

It is characteristic of Adrienne von Speyr to present this law of night simultaneously in the general form of faith experiences as such and in the particular form of mystical experience. To be sure, she does not identify the two; nevertheless, the mystical experience of night ultimately appears as the conscious unfolding, in particular contemplators, of a universal and fundamental state [*Grundbefindlichkeit*] of all Christian existence and all Christian contemplation. And while she does not deny the aspect of "purification", which is necessary for the contemplative, she accords a more important and more central place in the teaching of the dark night to the aspect of one's inclusion within the law of redeeming grace: because the Son on the Cross had to experience divine love and truth in the mode of abandonment and darkness, therefore the disciple of Jesus cannot be spared, in prayer, something significant along these lines.

The second fundamental principle is that of the *image*, which we could describe here as a concrete and tangible "correspondence of truth" between heaven and earth. Revelation is the revelation of heaven on earth—not through the production of words and images about the eternal, divine world, which only have to be dialectically eliminated or crossed out in the manner of "negative theology", but in a positivity, which can ultimately be understood only on the basis of love, and in love. Christ, the Son and Image of the Father, who became man, who died, but who was raised up and ascended into heaven, no longer crosses out the Word that he himself is, the Word that he unfolded in thousands of words, deeds, gestures and prayers, through his return to the Father. Indeed, he expands the sphere of images, in which genuine contemplation is alone able to unfold, until it includes the whole of creation. For the Creator, the Father, already laid the world upon the Son, and it needs the Son in order to be contemplated in its definitive meaning and to be interpreted.

Becoming incarnate, the Son takes hold of these image-laden intimations that rise up from below rather than descend from above, by filling these earthly images in his omnipotence with eternal meaning. Admittedly, this meaning is not accessible to the grasping sinner and unbeliever; in order to be received and taken in, it requires reverent faith and adoring contemplation, in which the earthly image opens up to its mysterious eternal content. And this content does not merely flash for a moment like a bolt of lightning, as it does for dialectical theology, but it is available in a certain stability in all of the images the Son has given: in the sacraments, God's truth is present in signs that are valid—indeed, they are definitive for the duration of the world; and God's heavenly Jerusalem, in which Christians receive a share in faith and prayer, is present in the Our Father and in all of the Son's words of prayer, just as it is in the liturgical words of the Church. The world as a whole, because of the presence of the incarnate Son who is the definitive Image of the Father, is transformed into a sort of sacrament of divine truth and love. Already by virtue of nature, the individual man is an image modeled on Christ (and through him on the triune God), and for this reason (as Paul explains in 2 Corinthians 3 and 4), he cannot understand or see himself merely in relation to himself; rather, only by looking to Christ can he become who he is, and only in Christ can he interpret and comprehend himself. In this way, the act of contemplative prayer becomes an indispensable act of human self-realization, which however is not something man affirms and practices in the first place for his own sake, but rather in obedience to God, who desires and needs human beings as disciples and followers of Christ. In the deepest sense, contemplation is the loving obedience that man gives as an answer to the Word of God.

Images are not there in order to be rejected and destroyed, buried in God's imageless abyss. In the Ascension, God's earthly image is seized and drawn up definitively to the Father, and the disciples, before they are sent back to Jerusalem by the angel, stand blessed and full of longing, filled and emptied at the same time on the Mount of Olives, staring after the One who has disappeared into God. The Transfigured One took their hearts with him up to God, and they will never again feel altogether at home in the temporal world, for that part of the world which they most loved is now with God. And this is why everything that they see on earth becomes transparent to heaven. The Holy Spirit, which the Son sends to them from heaven, kindles in them the fire of longing, in which every image on earth becomes radiant for heaven, for the everlasting life that springs up from triune love. To show this is the aim of the present little book.

— Hans Urs von Balthasar

# 1. The Idea in God

God looks upon God from all eternity. His life is this vision, in which the three Persons are transparent to one another and consummate and confirm their oneness in being in ever renewed exchanges of love. What God is in his eternal being is in the life of the three Persons a constant "now", an actually occurring event. Eternal love sees to it that their unity be manifest as unsurpassable and inexhaustible in every respect. God's contemplation of God is the most fruitful contemplation imaginable. It is an unending flow of giving and receiving, and at the same time it takes a direction, like the movement from the spring to the sea. The spring in God is so mighty that everything originates from it and no other prior origin can be sought behind it. Out of all the meanderings of its flowing love, it ultimately forms an ocean, which in its boundlessness illustrates God's infinity. What flows out, however, does not distance itself from the Father's spring, but is received and taken in by him. Ebb and flow, spring and sea, are all one in the endlessly flowing Godhead.

When God contemplates, he sees God, the eternal

God of action and contemplation: the God who performs actions and the God who receives them in order to contemplate them and who does not thereby
close them but rather opens them up. This opening
up of contemplation stems from the openness of the
one who contemplates. If a man loves a woman, he
will do everything he can to be transparent to the
one he loves and to grant her an insight into him, and
the beloved, the moment she perceives his love, will
do the same. In this way, a unity of being and of will
grows between them, though it does not violate their
personhood or eliminate the boundaries that distin-
guish them. Man remains man and woman remains
woman. The ultimate mystery of their person is not
laid bare; indeed, their reciprocal revelation to one
another serves only to deepen and quicken this mystery. Now, to be sure, we cannot speak of a deepen-
ing in God, for God is eternally the same. But he is
also the one who constantly and tirelessly produces
and receives the exchange of love. And this exchange
is not an idle exercise, but a brimming event.

If God the Father creates man with the cooperation
of the Son and the Spirit, then he guides man along
with all the rest of creation toward the Son. The
origin of all the contemplation in the world lies in
this movement of being guided toward the Son that
is willed by the Father. God wants to give to the
Son, whom he sees, all of those who do not yet see

him. And this gift is carried out in both directions from the beginning: God gives himself to man, but he also gives man to himself, so that man stands in the midst of a flowing exchange. Man does not grasp this exchange with his natural senses, but faith makes it visible at a level that remains withdrawn from human reason and its calculations. The believer, who stands outside of God's nature insofar as he is a creature, receives a share in God's interior world through faith: he who does not see the things of God on the basis of his nature receives a share in God's seeing. Faith is God's gift that opens up the world of God's inner life to him, and when it does, man sees this inner life, not as a distant and inaccessible illusion, like a Fata Morgana. Instead, God grants him a cognitive power out of his own vision so that man can contemplate him, in order to disclose the things that the Father offers to the Son and to the Spirit also to man, and to make them intelligible.

This gift of faith is therefore not a natural experience. When a person begins to contemplate and makes his first efforts at it, he may be disturbed at first that he experiences so little, and that the divine world that reveals itself to him appears to be so inaccessible precisely *in* its being revealed. He does not know where to look, where to go with his prayer, with his "vision" (for it is possible to use such a term even when there is nothing mystical about it);

he sees himself as a person who has stumbled into a foreign land and understands nothing about the inhabitants' language or the way one is supposed to act. Even so, the fact that he does not understand does not lead him to suppose that these people do not understand what they are saying to one another and that their behavior is bereft of all reason. It is only that he lacks the key to it. In the same way, the believer who stands at the beginning of contemplative prayer and looks on his attempts as useless and fruitless does not come to the conclusion that God himself is meaningless or that God is asking something meaningless of him; instead, he realizes that he must slowly accustom himself to the mores, language, customs and habits of God and of God's divine world.

In the beginning, nothing more is demanded of him than that he earnestly believe, and, as a believer, that he persevere and endure. And because faith means assenting to divine truth, he must hold open enough space in himself to be able to receive even the unfathomable aspect of God. He must acknowledge the validity of God's truth, not only in itself, but also for him, man. And he must make an effort, step by step, over and over again, to learn to be at home in the land of this divine truth. This is possible only in an act of the most profound obedience. Obedience and contemplation interpenetrate one another. It is altogether impossible that someone who is disobedient might practice genuine contemplation. Contemplative prayer is grounded in and fructified by obedience.

But even as a serious believer, man often experiences a distance, perhaps even a gaping chasm, between his natural world and God's world, so that this latter, measured in terms of his natural experience, often appears to be unreal and abstract. When he enters this darkness of faith, he will have to recall what it means to say that the world has been created in view of the Son. There is an eternal notion of the Creator present here, and these thoughts have for God the same density, concreteness and tangibleness from all eternity that the various sensual objects of our world have for us. God does not need to bring things into existence in order for them to be real for him. When he creates the world, he establishes a foundation underneath it to gather up his eternal will.

The creatures below man, which lack consciousness and will therefore never possess faith, will always remain unaware that they are ordered to the Son. But man is conscious, and he therefore ought to experience, through the grace of faith, the ultimate reason for which God created him. Even before he has awakened to faith, he has participated ontologically in the Father's world, for the temporal world was created as a function of an eternally concrete notion of the Father. And just as the reflective human being acquires an ultimate insight into what it means to be human the moment that he experiences in faith that he was created with a view to the incarnate God, so too the whole of time, which passes away, acquires a meaning for him the moment he experiences that it has been created out of an eternal duration and ordered to it, and that the two "ends" of time are dependent upon eternity. He thus sees that the whole duration of time is an analogy for the eternal, that it was conceived and created for man, so that he feels at home in existence, and that the question he puts to God does not shatter from the outset upon an inaccessible eternity, but finds in countable time an adequate medium for a multifaceted reply. Along with the space in which man is placed, the time that is vouchsafed to him is something suited to his finite essence, wherein he now receives precisely the space and time to reflect on his essence and to recognize that the Creator has intended for this essence to find its fulfillment beyond finite spaces and times: it is destined to lead into God's world. And precisely insofar as the measurable and graspable points beyond itself to the ungraspability of God, it reveals its own meaning. To lead into God is not to come to a violent end, but a new and sheltering beginning. Man's deepest mystery comes to light in the resurrection of the body, for it shows that human space leads into heaven, and ephemeral time leads into eternity. In this way the exchange of love within God opens up to the world: as an exchange between heaven and earth, God and man. And if man experiences something of this supreme mystery in faith, what he sees is not something alienating and distant. Rather, he receives the most intimate reality of being and the meaning of things and of himself as matter for contemplation.

God is man's creator, judge, redeemer and beatifier. The series of properties that God shows to man in his relationship to him could be enumerated *ad infinitum*. He is constantly revealing new sides of his infinite being to his creation. He allows man to approach him from every possible angle, to recognize his deeds, and through them to enrich his image of God. And he expects man to assimilate these ever new features into his concept of God: this is what the human mind's answer ought to be to God's constantly new revelation. And a new adoration ought to result from the new conception. A particular paradigm will be offered at every moment to the reflective spirit as a truth and reality to be contemplated; he is permitted to analyze this concept into its elements, and to enjoy them and enrich himself through them in his contemplation, in order that he draw nearer to God—to a God who has desired from all time to be recognized by man in all of his revelations. The Father goes so far as to reveal even the relationship he has with the Son and the Spirit, as it exists eternally in heaven, through the signs, words, and gestures of the incarnate Son, so that, from God's eternal contemplation of God, man might receive not merely a vague intimation, but a genuine insight into God, and a sense for him. The ones who are closest to God ought to learn the most; but no one should think that he was passed over, that he was forgotten or dismissed when the invitations were given, for the Father is the Creator of all men and has ordered all to the Son; the Son has redeemed all men, and the Spirit, who blows where he will, heeds no boundaries.

The Son revealed God chiefly to man. To be sure, he suffered his Cross before the eyes of his Father, who perceived every one of the Son's hidden thoughts; but he suffered the Cross no less before the eyes of men, so that they could contemplate his suffering and thereby be strengthened in their prayer and in their faith. The immediate proximity of the Cross ought to bring them into its mysteries of reconciliation and redemption and thus also to show them who they are and how distant they had been. As the Son, who takes away all sins, bridges over this distance, it should become clear to them how great this chasm truly was, the chasm that represents the essential condition of a sinful creature, seen with the eyes of faith.

If God the Father allows the whole of human history to unfold before his unchanging eyes, we also get a glimpse of his idea of the man who contemplates. Adam's contemplation had a different inner form than Abraham's did, and this latter's differs from that of Job or of David or of the New Testament. But the Cross stands at the center of this development: it is from the perspective of the Cross that we can interpret both the contemplation of the first Christians and that of the last Jews who looked for the coming of the Messiah in their contemplation. Indeed, we can interpret the contemplation of all Christians even up to the present day, and of all Jews all the way to the beginning.

But there is one feature of contemplation that the Cross brings most particularly into view: obedience. Precisely here where the Son, who is led to the Cross in obedience to the Father, lost the Father and cries out to him as one abandoned, a new spring of contemplation begins to flow: the night of prayer. This night is given only to a few, who are meant to be united with the Lord in a particularly intimate way, but it has been distributed over and over again down through the centuries, in order that the cry of abandonment might find its way to the unique cry of the Son, so that it might be received by him, and draw one's gaze to him. And this same spring that begins to flow on the Cross opens up the meaning of obedience within the Church. The individual would not have been able to remain in faith for the entire duration of his life if the Son had not founded the Church, giving his Cross to her in such a way that she could administer it for all future generations. Through the Church, the Cross becomes for every age the distinctive mark of the presence of the Son's life among us and for that reason the presence of the contemplation of his life and suffering as the origin of God's new and eternal Covenant with man.

It is just as true to say that the Son's cry of death is the end of his vision, as it is to claim that it is the beginning of all human contemplation, a beginning that constantly restarts in God so that God's will might become manifest all over again. It is as if the spring has been flowing for ages and bringing forth the great rivers that stretch out to the sea along visible paths and roundabout ways, while the very first beginning, the original spring itself, is able to be seen only afterward. The spring lies in the Son, it lies in the Cross, it arises from the abyss of the mortal dread of the one abandoned by the Father. This dread is the first real perception of what sin means in truth, the first perception of man's true condition before God, and at the same time it is a perception of what the greatness of God's love takes upon itself, what it bridges over, what the Son's sacrifice lifts up and renews as a new creation. As believers, we stand before the contemplation of the Cross like children who learn only in later years what their father had in mind for them, what their mother, and their various teachers, had in mind for them, and who suddenly in all of this, in the alternations of punishment and reward, encouragement and restraint, catch sight of the outlines of a unified plan that was conceived for their good.

The unity of the triune God and his eternal plan of salvation has always existed; but its full and central revelation occurs in the Cross. Here it becomes clear what God desires for man, what man receives as a gift, but also what he must be and do. The Son is obedient unto death, and he keeps his eyes fixed on the Father until his vision gives out in the night —and it is in this night that the highest point, the extremity of God's love for man and the extremity of man's obedience to God is revealed. Here, contemplation has its concrete origin: it is here that God's grace of redemption becomes perceptible, but also the fruitfulness of man's consent; and just as contemplation takes its nourishment in the reception of grace, it is also nourished by sharing in the act of obedience.

God created man as an individual, and thus the Son too suffers alone on the Cross for each individual, which links each individual directly to the suffering Lord. One of the consequences of this, however, is that each individual contemplates according to the measure of his unique personal existence. This does not encroach upon the fullness of the gospel in its objective and universally binding validity. But within this full and complete form, each contemplating person must seek to understand the word that is meant for him, the plan that is forged for him, the suffering that is undertaken for him personally. Contemplation must be ecclesial and universal, and it must endeavor to extend to the breadth of God's plan for the world; but it must also be personal and unique, and must not forget that each person stands before God as someone who is unique and loved with a particular love, someone who has been known and entrusted with a particular task.

Both because God's word is universal and because it is personal, it will always have infinitely more to offer to the one contemplating than he is able to grasp. The word can be brief and unequivocal; but at the same time there is in the word "more than all the books in the world can contain"; fruitful contemplation will recognize that new meaning and new connections will constantly flow out from it and be born from it. Everything universally true becomes personal, and it thereby suddenly receives a completely new face, even if a person thought he had already understood it. And everything personal necessarily becomes catholic and universal, and only then does it exhibit its entire breadth. Man is man, and word is word: this is the way man sees things; but man is not

Everyman and not every word is the same. And if the Word has been with God from the very beginning and if the Word *is* God, then the Word lays claim to every person who encounters it in prayer, in and beyond all of his powers. Indeed, the Word, which is God, lays hold of man and equips him with new powers—faith, hope and love—which enable him to grasp the Word and which even expand him to such an extent that, at the limit, he receives something of God's idea of contemplation.

Human beings, who were strangers to each other at first, but who became connected through an idea, an aspiration, or a hope, possess a certain mutual understanding. A like-minded person is not merely a person one likes, but someone in whom one sees the fire of one's own idea. A kind of agreement holds sway, that seeks to grow through communication, that binds together the two who are united and that allows them to have a share in one another. Though it be in an infinitely subtle manner (because it is mediated through the Son's grace), faith forms precisely this sort of bond between believers, and thus places the contemplation of the Son's obedience, his words, and his entire Incarnation, in a new and fruitful light. The one idea of contemplation allows itself to be newly contemplated from the perspectives of various aspects of revelation: from the perspective of the Church and her fixed boundaries, from the perspective of the Church's inner Bridal mystery, from the perspective of Christ's brotherhood with us, his eternal Sonship in relation to the Father, and from the perspective of all the truths of revelation. The Father places something of the plan he has for man in every revealed truth. And in every part of revelation there is the whole God, just as the whole Son is in every part of the mystery of his earthly life.

Therefore the many people who contemplate in prayer God's various mysteries or the Son's earthly life meet in the constantly overwhelming and inexhaustible object of their contemplation, and they become reciprocally open to one another in this object. There are wide expanses in God and in Jesus' life, however, that lie beyond the scope of contemplation, because they are not disclosed in an immediate way but are at most accessible indirectly and inferentially (as for example the details of the thirty years of the hidden life of Jesus): these areas allow one to see clearly that the object always transcends those who contemplate and that they will never be able to exhaust it. The object of contemplation not only unites the contemplators with itself but also binds them all together within its overflowing unity, in a manner that is perhaps even deeper than any immediate conversation could ever do. In this way, the person who contemplates becomes a particularly lively member of the community of believers.

# 2. Perceiving God's Will

Adam was able to understand the words the Creator addressed to him; in fact, they were clear and unambiguous. He did not have to pore over them in order to get more out of them than he had initially understood. But when sin arose between man and God, Adam was forced to learn how to make excuses. These excuses were words of untruth, of distance and alienation, words reflecting a desire no longer to understand; they raised a line of separation between God's word and its being understood. The immediate contact was broken off, the receiving organ damaged, the feeling dulled, and God's will henceforth seemed uncertain and obscure.

In the Old Covenant, those who were commissioned by God and the believers who followed them sought to reinstate this [original] relationship as far as possible in order to make it clear what God wanted. But they were directed to make use of hints, reflections, and comparisons in order to have some sense of how a sinner ought to approach the one who is totally pure. It was no longer the un-mediated relationship between God and the man who had just sprung forth the Creator in his original innocence;

instead, the relationship was sullied by all the detours and subterfuges of untruth. The vision of the highest truth was moreover so obscured that man preferred to associate with other men as a way toward this truth, rather than immediately with God. Only occasionally did he let his guard down; for the most part, he put up intermediate stages and mediating authorities and enclosed even God within these man-made walls. Man tried to restore the clarity and precision that God's word lost by replacing it with the pseudo-clarity of human words. And when God's voice rang out and the prophets had to proclaim it, it was no mean task for them to make God's will intelligible also to others. But there could be no doubt that the people understood. The ones who were called and designated to proclaim often had to invent their own speech in order to make the message intelligible to sinners. The naked word would never have reached them.

But then God's Word, who had been with him from all eternity and who was the Son, allowed himself to become man, so that the Father would have a man who could perceive his will and accept it in a proper way, without the need for mediation or translation. And because of him a genuine perception was to take its place again on earth among other men as well. The Word made flesh spoke to man; he formulated sentences filled with divine meaning for believers, he gave instructions for living properly and allowed the Creator to be seen in what

he did and what he said. He was not only a man
but also a Way, a way that one could follow and
that led back to the Father. He allowed himself to
become transparent in pure service and obedience
so that the human spirit could once again become
transparent to the Father. When the apostle begs the
Lord, "Show us the Father!" and the Son answers,
"Whoever sees me sees the Father", it becomes immediately clear that his existence has given rise to a
point of intersection between the Father and man,
a point wherein they can encounter one another in
an immediate way. Admittedly, man does not realize that he is genuinely able to see the Father in the
Son; he has been unacquainted with this immediate
contact with God for so long that he fails to grasp
the new and unsuspected access to the Father that
he is being offered.

But the Son also teaches man a new way to pray.
He showed him how to say the Father's prayer. He
also showed him his own prayer as a Son, a prayer
that grows out of his vision and perfectly grasps the
Father's will, a prayer that has appropriated this will
and can thus become the praying man's model for
how the triune God's will ought to be understood
in the world. Here man can be raised up beyond
his own level and brought onto God's level, and he
can even acquire a grasp of God's eternal will. He
does not grasp this with his natural reason, but with
his prayer-reason. Prayer carries him beyond himself
and places him in this grasp, without him becoming

aware of it. He is placed on the path of obedience, and obedience allows him to receive a share of God's omniscience. In a certain respect, "Thy will be done" means also that man receives a sense for this will, even if he is unable to express it in words; he is brought over into this will, even if he does not understand how to interpret it; he carries out this will, even if he does not know where it is taking him. And yet not everything remains obscure to his understanding, because this will leads him ever deeper into the will.

Being led into the will is something that happens through love. Even if man does not know what it means, he nevertheless understands that his obedience is a response to God's love and that this love embraces him all along the way. He is led by love into the mystery of God's triune love. And it may happen that inconceivable marvels become revealed to him in this, there may be moments in which he comes to see himself as one chosen and loved, and God makes him worthy to consecrate himself to him. But this consecration is not something he can understand in earthly terms, because two spheres come together here which cannot be brought into a fixed and unambiguous relationship. One sphere contains the things that God wants to show, in such a way that the thing shown becomes perfectly meaningful and transparent for the one who experiences it; it gets arranged in his faith, it becomes a part of

his love, it inspires him to a renewed commitment
or an increased prayer; it also shows him how the
prayer of love of neighbor is meant for him, what
God expects from him in this respect, how certain
lines of the following of Christ have been traced out
for him. But at the same time the love of God and
obedience to him and the being led into his otherwise closed world (insofar as it has not been revealed
through words and experiences) consist in realities
that are and remain invisible, because they have their
place within the exchange of triune love. This invisibility does not necessarily have to be identified with
the Little Thérèse's "voyage underground" and with
her "tunnel", because the one who has been taken
up may be accompanied by a powerful certainty and
security. But it can nevertheless seem to him that he
has become blind, that he has lent out his eyes, indeed that his eyes have become superfluous, because
God acts and sees so much on his behalf that he has
been relieved of the obligation of seeing for himself.

He cannot remain in God's will without prayer.
And this prayer will consist in part of what is ordinary and performed out of duty, it will consist of
words that make sense to the one who prays, familiar thought processes, petitions, promises of self-gift,
which he knows and which have been entrusted to
him over time. But at the same time it is as if this
prayer were lifted up [*aufgehoben*], no longer spoken
by him, but rather taken over by a love in which

he has received a share: the Church's love for God, God's love for the Church or for individual people. The words can no longer be grasped individually; their meaning has become unimportant, because a greater reality has gotten the upper hand, an invisible reality that encompasses him, and that somehow crosses and covers the inner mysteries of God with invisibility.

Things may also happen in the love between human beings which flow into one another as if all defenses were down. Man passes beyond limitations; indeed, he is even lifted over walls—some that he knows but also some that he does not know—so that the share that was intended for him not be diminished, so that he need not do the measuring himself; he need not draw his own border limits; he need not have the responsibility of tracing out his own path. He passes unencumbered, because he is being led. Thus, a small child finds his way through the most difficult stray paths when he is able to walk holding his father's hand. From his own perspective, he may be aware only that there is a house here, and that there are other houses further on, and that at this corner or the next there is something familiar; but that is as far as he can make out, because the distances and the pathways and the connections are not clear to him. The child thus learns to have more trust in the father and his guidance. The man who prays has a similar experience, which is often difficult to put into words but is no less real, an experience that brings him to a stricter obedience, to an increase of prayer, an experience that lends him new strength, which clearly does not come from himself, and a certainty in faith, which is indispensable for his self-gift and his service. Before, he had no idea how necessary this certainty was. It is only now that he experiences it, only now that it has become clear to him in this sense.

A Christian, who has been praying in a contemplative way for a certain time, and who does it with joy even if he has not grasped its full meaning, who has perhaps begun to contemplate out of respect for another person who showed him this kind of prayer, needs a long time before he begins to see how much he is already connected with God's world and God's truth, how far along the path he has already come, a path that never goes backward. The same is true in the perception of God's will: it cannot happen in any other way than by submitting oneself, by giving one's a priori Yes, one's assent, which in the world of prayer always occurs before the question has become entirely clear. Thus man is drawn ever more deeply into God's truth and his design. He was already inside, as a part, before he realized it; without knowing what the consequences would be, he submitted himself, and this submission placed him so much at God's disposal that he, God's instrument, has now received a hidden knowledge; he has become one who knows even about things that have not at this point been given to him to investigate. And since he has been carried beyond limitations in prayer, he should no longer try to put back the boundary-stones, the limitations and fences, once again in the everyday world, in the modesty of the task he must carry out, which requires his attention in another way and which requires the engagement of other capacities. He ought to remain in the trust that corresponds to this transcendence; he ought to know that the path that God calls him to walk is a particular path, which is always meaningful for God as long as man obeys. To introduce human measures would be to weaken prayer, to use the hours that belong to God for one's own ego and thus to steal from God and to bring his displeasure upon oneself. For God cannot repeat what he intended to do, or something similar, and thus the following of him suffers as a result.

But once man has obeyed, he now knows something new: he knows that a human being can become aware of God's will; that this particular following of God is part of his will. And he thereby also learns what matters to God above all other things: that more love be given to him and more love be given to one's neighbors. Every will of God that man is permitted to experience in some way can be brought back to love.

# 3. Light

Faith is like a light that shines out in all directions and allows things to show themselves for what they are—no longer as they were before redemption or as it pleased man's imagination to see them, but objectively. The light of faith comes from God. Just as he said, "Let there be light!", and there was light, and he saw that the light was good, so too does he bestow faith: in a streaming fullness and in a manner that he finds good.

The divine vision, which the Son has of the Father, stands above every faith. It is the knowledge that the Son has possessed from all eternity as God, and which inundates his humanity in a unique way, a knowledge that binds him both to the Father and to the Spirit and distinguishes him from them as a Person. By contrast, the gift the triune God gives to man in the grace of faith may indeed have a similarity to the reciprocal vision of the three Persons in God and to the incarnate Son's vision of the Father, but it is the sort of seeing that befalls man in his pilgrim state; it is a relationship that God establishes on his own terms and gives to man, and at the same time allows the believer to give in return.

This faith is such that, when it is alive, it is like a continually fed flame, out of which, in a continuous and unpredictable stream, spring new effects of light, sparks and flashes. These sparks and flashes illuminate things in a different way; they cast living shadows, and bring shifting contours out of the half-dark. The image of God and of the world that a living faith conveys is one that is in motion to the greatest extent, an image that can never be nailed down or used up: it imposes itself, it seeks to be seen, it uncovers ever new treasures, it lets itself be caught in many faces and yet is never confined, because other faces lie behind these waiting their turn, unsuspected elements enter into the picture, and the whole thus suddenly takes on a new hue. One could also compare faith to a game that God conducts, in which there are constantly new twists and connections: it is never the same thing twice. In spite of all this, faith is as stable and enduring as the light of the sun, under which the day goes through all of its changes. The time that fades and everything that transpires in it do nothing to change faith. It is the fulfillment of the many promises that lie in temporality but are fulfilled by God. One cannot expect man to be capable on his own of coming up with new and valid images of his faith in the course of time as it passes away. But God gives him such images, and these images make contact with ephemeral time without being absorbed or swept away by it.

Light is also such that it always shows and communicates something that lasts in what it conveys even if its rays reveal something new at every moment. Just as it is the case that people were not created according to a fixed schema, but rather each one shows his own personality, which changes according to laws of growth, and can perceive its changes, so too light has its own laws, which belong to God, and which enliven the believer's whole relationship to God. In paradise, God went about at determined times that were not unknown to Adam. He knows: now is God's hour. However, he lost this knowledge for the most part after the Fall. The relationship has to be restored, God's word has to be understood again; grace must place the word back into a new light for man, a light that he failed to notice until now, but which will illuminate the word once more.

It is not for nothing that the star, which led the believers to the Child, should be a light; it illuminates the first adoration of Christ. The Son came into the world as the light of the Father, as the bearer of the Father's image and also of the image of man, whom the Father had created. Whatever he does or says is bathed in this light, which is at the same time the light of the fulfilled promise—insofar as it was in part already known—and yet as the full light introduces everything new, eternal, and unhoped-for.

God kindles the light of faith in man; but man, as the bearer of this light, must keep the flame of faith and of the word burning within him. He is responsible for what he has received; it must not flicker, but shed light; and in order for it to give light, man must make use of it, and the service he undertakes is the service of God. Serving God cannot occur in the closed sphere of mundane ordinariness, but needs God's fresh air (just as the light needs it in order to burn)—air which blows from God each day anew and which illuminates the knowledge of the Father, Son and Spirit ever anew. A man who perceives a word from his God in the light of faith knows precisely that this word, which today overwhelms him and throws him off balance, must henceforward retain its power for him. He knows that this experience makes him responsible for the light that this word casts; that other people ought to see it too and order their actions in view of it. In order for the light to burn and to be seen and persist in its responsibility toward God, it needs two things: the movement that God gives to it, the direction in which he sends it forth, but also the living faith that it takes hold of and cultivates. And thus believers, whom Paul calls children of the light, stand continuously in the light. Even those to whom the dark night has been given are not permitted to distance themselves from the light's rays; against their own knowledge and their own will, they have to pass the light on as those who have been illuminated, they must continue to grasp God's word as those who respond.

The whole prayer of faith can be compared to a living light. God may grant it in what appears to be a scanty measure for days at a time—even to those who are not in the night of prayer—and suddenly new words from God leap out, new meanings and new demands of faith, from the half-darkness. These words were already there hidden in God and in objective faith, but the light of faith sent by God happens to fall on them in this hour of grace, in order to lend them visibility.

If a person does not believe, then he must give all of the Christian concepts and all concepts of love a content that he composes out of his own materials, if he happens to take any interest in these concepts. But he always ends up turning away again from what he himself has created, because it remains in a twilight, and does not become sufficiently supple. Deception can entice him to want to get closer to truth through the experience of sin. But he does not realize that he only gets further from it and that God's word gets swallowed up by darkness because he desecrates it.

But if he begins to believe and possesses a number of his own concepts, he takes them out, somewhat shyly, and places them in the light of faith. Doing so, he experiences shock and stands amazed at how radiant they suddenly become, how they express something new. These concepts show a definitiveness that belonged to them long ago before he had taken up with them, a definitiveness that comes from God himself and never fails—whether it concerns concepts of love or punishment, temporality or eternity —to reveal something about his eternal love. Everything is now charged with value, a value whose power of radiance comes only from faith. Thus, a person who has just come to faith can have the experience that, when using old and familiar words, he is suddenly blinded and sent reeling by a lightning bolt, unable to grasp what is happening to him and believing he has learned a foreign language. Like one who has made a discovery, he can take out word after word of the new language, testing each one, contemplating it, placing it in the light of faith and delighting in his insight and penetration.

But the new light is not there simply for one's enjoyment; it also means carrying out tasks and thus taking on new ones. Every promise that the Son fulfilled, the Son took into his awareness of the obligation of mission. He searched the words of the Old Covenant, which he had to fulfill, he chose the images for his parables that he wished to fill with Christian meaning; he thought through where he ought to place his foot so that he would leave behind traces, which his Father foreknew and which could have led the Jews to see him as the Promised One. In this way, he gave *his* meaning to the concept of fulfillment for all those who are somehow touched by it; and this form does not pass away.

The believer comes across traces of the Son everywhere in the words and concepts of Scripture, which he makes his own. The words themselves take charge of leading him; perhaps he is not aware at first that he is being led, because the first impression, the shock, that the words provoke in him is too strong. He first has to recover to a certain extent, and make peace with the force that has come upon him. But he himself does not dictate the terms of this peace; the conditions lie with God. He remains in all of this the one who surrendered, the one who was conquered. But no matter how hard the task may be, no matter how difficult the path, how imperfect his following, from now on the love of the triune God remains visible to him everywhere. He experiences this presence as a constant streaming forth of the light in the ebullience of the source.

God has initiated a new love relationship even with him and expects that he will radiate the new love. And though he now has reached the way of the Son, this is not a general, well-traveled way, but the path of a special love that has never belonged to anyone else, just as the Son on the Cross bore the sins of all as a particular person.

If before, when he was an unbeliever or a lukewarm Christian, he occupied himself with his own concepts within the confines of his ego, this new experience, the insight into the new fullness, is something that does not affect him alone but that passes through the center of his living relationship to God. Thus, from this moment on, he no longer experiences even the heaviest burden as something private but always as a burden that originally lay upon the Cross. And thus, from the center of this relationship and of all Christian concepts, a new word emerges: "With". He will love with others. He will be one who is loved along with others. He will bear things with others. He will have a share, with others, in everything that the Lord is. Not as an outsider, or at most one who undergoes things as he stands on the sidelines, but rather as one who is expected to co-operate in the Lord's earthly work. Henceforward, all of the words and concepts bear the trace of this "with"; they have a connection to it, they take on their full meaning only when they are interpreted as words in the dialogue between God and man. Now they belong to the salt that God uses to season his food; and this salt is not permitted to go stale. The light is not merely a general light, it is in the deepest sense a common light, one that grants community. It not only shows God's new world, it allows one to participate in it.

The believer will not thus be forced to play a role that is foreign to him, or to be involved in an adventure that is too much for him. The question that God addresses to him, the question that was meant for him personally and made visible to him, never goes away, so that his response may likewise always remain alive. The little word "with" loses nothing of its power: what it was yesterday, it ought still to be today, so that it can also be the same tomorrow.

And the "with", which is a mystery of love, now comprehends even time: temporal duration becomes a share in eternal life. That which cannot be grasped and held fast belongs to that which has been grasped and held by God from all eternity. The day that draws to a close belongs to heaven's dawn; but the earthly task that it holds, its practical and concrete task, thereby loses nothing of its urgency; it must be carried out, here and now, without hesitation or reflection. The little that man is able to do possesses its full weight in the response he gives to God. The response demands his entire life, because he is able to give it again each day. But the task, which was born in the absolute, knows and follows the rhythms of the day. Man must not forget its origin in God and its eternal totality; he must not affirm it with only a part of himself, leaving the rest to fall into the habits and laziness of earthly life. God needs the entire man for the entire task; the response of man's spirit to God's Spirit demands the whole of him, body and soul. It needs to be realized concretely in time. And if man believes in the resurrection of the body, then he ought to be able to understand why the whole of him is demanded: his bodily life on earth carries out a task that ought to be deposited as a whole into the safekeeping of eternal life. Once God desires to have something as a whole in eternity, it must already be offered to him as a whole in time.

# 4. Shadow

In his following of Christ, man draws sustenance from God's question, which invited him and to which he attempted to give his answer. This assent does not belong to him; if it were his alone, it would have been too weak. It would have been subjected to all of the inessential events of his daily life. As his experience teaches him, it would have been constantly overwhelmed by sin and estrangement. God the Son gave the Father an ultimately valid assent to his mission, a divine Yes that was without any weakness. And through the pre-redemption, he brought it about that Mary's Yes, too, would be immaculate, undiminished, made in a childlike trust and untainted by the temptations and fears to which it was exposed. It remained firm, because it was spoken entirely in God, because God himself gave it in such a way that the Mother experienced the strength of her own word not in herself, but solely in the Son. The Yes of the apostles and all the other disciples has a connection to this and draws sustenance from the power of the Yes given by the Son and the Mother. No believer's consent would have any validity if it were not contained within and borne by this original two-fold assent.

Peter says Yes, but he also says No. He falters. In him, we get a glimpse of the shadow that is found in every sinner's consent and weakens so much of his prayer. His consent would be completely impotent and invalid if a seed of the Son's consent did not lie within it, and if the Father were not able to look upon this unclouded consent. And the Mother's consent in its service directs things toward the Son; this is the paradigm of the Church's consent, which dwells within every personal consent.

Nevertheless, man is free in his acceptance. But if he says Yes, he knows in his heart of hearts that it is not he that brought about this Yes, but the grace within him. He surrenders himself to grace, and grace undertakes to lead him to God. To surrender oneself to grace in this way is a risk, but man accepts it because the Son stands surety for him. And he knows: he must now be holy. If he were to be granted the capacity to see into the souls of the many who have wagered this Yes without being holy, he would receive a profound shock; he would see this word submerged under a flood of Nos, into which it sinks ever deeper, up to the point that the person perhaps even loses the feeling for the impotence of his consent.

The Yes one speaks can come only from prayer. It does not need in every respect to be one's own prayer; there is above all the triune relationship of love in heaven, which is the foundation and pre-condition for all prayer in the world. There is the Church's treasury of prayer that lies somewhere be-tween heaven and earth. There are the prayers of the countless people in the Church, many of whom offer their petitions for the success of others' follow-ing, perhaps because they were unable to achieve the complete following of the Lord that they had longed for themselves. There is the powerful prayer of the saints, of the many who walk the path of discipleship of the Lord; this prayer is placed at God's disposal in such a way that he allows it to be administered by the Church and supplies this person or that with so much of this prayer that the person is suddenly and for no apparent reason transformed from one who is hesitating to one who gives his consent. So much that, from this moment on, he receives, not only a passive share in the Church's objective power of prayer, which had actively influenced him, but he himself becomes co-active in this fullness of prayer, he rounds it out and strives to become a means to its continued existence.

Such a person has a profound awareness that the light given to him has cast away many shadows in him, but that other shadows are still present. Per-haps the shadows of his hesitation, fear and uncer-tainty have been overcome, which threw up obsta-cles that rendered him unfit to serve God; but there remain shadows that he must drive away through his own effort: shadows that serve to bring him to a greater humility, even shadows that have newly arisen through failings in his discipleship, shadows that could darken him in certain moments and that seem to have more power over him than even his consent, more power than the grace he encountered, indeed more power than all the things that make up his life, because he realizes that he would have to overcome himself, perhaps tomorrow, perhaps some other time, just not today, because today he doesn't have the courage for it. Perhaps God wills that, in his following, he remain constantly aware of the burden of the consequences of original sin, or perhaps also of the sins of others, whose weakness has been placed on his shoulders.

His prayer and his contemplation will have to bear the darkness of these shadows: all the lukewarmness or boredom, all the doubts or scruples, all the questions that assail him, whether he really has been called, whether he is capable of giving God the response he expects.

God receives the consent and the prayer of his own through the Son and the Church. The Son gives the one who prays a place within his own prayer, and the Church gives him something of her powers of "mobility": something of her unbounded, indeed free prayer, which has been offered at the same time to this one or that one, to one person or to many. It often happens that one who prays realizes that he is being carried by a strength whose source is unknown to him, he finds words on his lips that are not his words, he seeks and acquires a relationship to God that is different from the one he was looking for; he makes use of a foreign good in order to be able to transform his own paths, foreign thoughts and words lend themselves, which come to him unexpectedly, so that he may adore the divine Word. Souls that believe they were not meant for contemplation meet with treasures in their prayer that have belonged to the Church forever: liturgical formulas, biblical prayer words that have been entrusted to the souls for ages, so long that they no longer hoped to get anything new out of them, words that seemed so worn out that they come across as empty, dry, practically meaningless—but now they have been purified overnight, they have been filled up again and made fresh and now radiate the entire miracle of the first consent. Every piece of dust has been blown away, everything has become as young as on the day of the first commission. Faith has recovered its original meaning. The consent, which had grown so faded, now seems so new, it is as if it were being spoken by someone else—and in fact it is! And yet a person can let himself be carried by this word more securely, more familiarly and trustingly, than if it were his own word, in the firm certainty that it is not he, the one praying, who is carrying and forming the word, but vice versa. New life flows forth from prayer, while the old life is taken away and placed at a distance from him. He had intended to follow the Lord, but this following has trailed after him. He had intended to pray, but prayer has absorbed him; faith clings to him so tightly that he can do nothing but move himself within its form, and the greater this faith is—such as the saints' faith, the Mother's faith, and ultimately the participation in the Son's vision of the Father—the more tightly it clings to the one who prays.

The shadow does not go away; the shadow of the whole sinful world, of original sin, of personal sins and mistakes remains alive and unable to be killed. But a new light floods even the shadow, because the one who prays, whether he knows it or not, participates in the event of the Cross and finds himself on the path back from the Cross to the life of discipleship.

The power to follow the Lord comes from the Lord's consent. Man hands himself over to the Lord in an act of trust, of powerful faith, in a gift of self that does not care to count the costs and rests above all on the fact that the Lord does not abandon his own. For the future, a person reckons more with hiddenness than with shadows and suffering. But if the believer contemplates the Lord's life, which was from first to last a life of prayer, then he cannot fail to see that the most powerful prayers are indeed those trickling words that the Lord speaks on the Cross: words of the highest suffering, which express the highest self-gift. Words that bear witness to what cannot be put into words, what he is undergoing. The one who prays takes in these words, and if he has resolved to follow the Lord in truth, then along with these words he assimilates a quality of the Lord's suffering on the Cross, which he does not determine himself and which nevertheless inevitably casts the shadow of the Cross over his existence.

If he too now suffers, then it is no longer the sort of suffering that he can identify and characterize in a basic way; he no longer suffers from a particular sin that he committed, from a sickness that has been laid upon him, from a certain feeling or angst that assails him; he now learns anonymous suffering, which resists any diagnosis, and is joined to the Lord in a way that defies boundaries. The Lord's Cross cannot be divided and broken up by the contemplator into delimited phases, any more than the suffering of the one who follows can be clearly determined. For this reason, his prayer must flow into the Lord's prayer: he offers it in an act of love that does not calculate, does not determine and also does not wish to be determined. To be sure, the Lord suffers for each sin individually, and he knows it; he sees open before him not only the hearts of those who stand under the Cross, but the hearts of all those who are co-responsible for his suffering. The one who follows the Lord is spared from such an insight; out of the entire substance of the suffering, he receives a single particle. This particle cannot be defined; he knows, in faith, only that the Lord set it aside for him and now entrusts him with it. Naturally, there is also suffering that can be defined in terms of its origin and end, but even this becomes primarily a part of the anonymous Christian totality, in order to be a resource for future use. And the believer to whom this determinate suffering has been given, must persist in his prayer and in his entire following of the Lord in anonymity, both in relation to what concerns himself—he is simply one person in prayer among a thousand, in the Church's ranks— and in relation to what concerns the mission to this particular suffering.

It is impossible that the disciple's prayer should always be the radiant prayer of thanksgiving of the child coddled by grace; it must also be able to accept the features of the Lord's suffering to the extent that Lord wishes it to. This belongs to the shadow that stretches over a Christian's life, but also to its brightness, because the shadow that he bears casts light on other shadows. And this bearing of the shadow is limited to time, just as the Lord's Cross too passed away. The Son calls out to the Father: "Why hast thou forsaken me!", the one who prays experiences hours in which he would like to call out the same thing; but he knows that he must simply hold on for the time being, because the Lord's Cross has in fact passed. He knows that he also sees brightness in the darkness: the shadows do not become for him entirely formless, they change shape, they are subject to a law that God administers.

Whether he speaks or keeps silent, the Son is always eloquent in relation to the Father; the Father always understands him and always agrees with him. The Son wishes to form a similar unity with the one who prays. Whether he speaks or is silent, whether he is giving thanks or suffering, the person who prays ought to be in unison with him. Being understood by the Lord and his love is the constant of this relationship, and the one who prays clings to this in order to come into accord. But when is there perfect accord?

And yet it is not only the prayer that comes expressly from the Cross and returns to it that is fraught with suffering; a moment of suffering already lies in the discrepancy between the human word in prayer and its full meaning in heaven. If the Christian disciple repeats the Lord's words of the Our Father, he does so in the awareness that every word carries much less significance in his mouth than it ought to carry. He hardly knows who the Father is;

he has even less of a sense of what heaven means, and still less what the Father's kingdom is. Nevertheless, he calls God Father, he mentions heaven, and he hopes for the kingdom. He dares to do this even though he remains submerged. Like a pupil facing a difficult text, though he understands individual words, the meaning of complete sentences in the meantime escapes him. The discrepancy comes through so painfully because there dwells among us one who knows the meaning of the words, to whom their entire content, their entire fullness is present, indeed in whom they in fact have their fullness. The others are sinners, and the sins that they have committed, as well as those that others have committed, drag them down to a level at which the word cannot achieve parity with its meaning. This is suffering. And yet this suffering was borne by the Son on the Cross, and what men experience are its reflections that flow from the Cross but also reflect back to it, while the Son underwent the original suffering alone.

But there is also a grace that keeps the shadow of suffering at a distance, that postpones it for later; this is a grace that arises from the "consummation" of the Cross. The Lord suffered through the whole suffering so that he can invite his own to a joyful discipleship in the security of faith. He will grant them a genuine participation in the Cross only once the longing for it has awakened in them, only when their love has grown to such a point that they no longer want to leave him alone for a moment, not even while he is on the Cross. A friend wants to experience and share with his friend as much as possible. He feels at many times that he has only a dim grasp of his friend's inner experiences, especially his suffering; it is like a gap in the light, which belongs to the whole, but has not yet been communicated in all of its detail. It is possible that the friend does not want to speak about it, that he doesn't want to open himself in this particular matter. But the Lord does not allow us to set boundaries. He wants to give everything, since he has in fact given his entire life for his own. But, out of love, he does not give man a share in everything right at the outset, because he does not wish to overburden him and does not want the adventure of Christian life to appear so heavy to him. He fills man's prayer with love and adoration, but in prayer he places him unexpectedly and, so to speak, as a matter of course before truths for which the man has not yet reached a maturity, before phrases that he repeats in a certain willingness without being able to take them perfectly seriously. The Lord has taken them seriously, and felt their weight, in his place; he has passed these phrases through his suffering love. Now they have become accessible, repeatable, even for the most hesitant. When they see these truths float through their prayer as shadows, then something stirs in them—as a yearning in love —and draws them toward discipleship.

# 5. The Night

When the Father distinguished day from night in his creation of the world, the act that separated them involved a judgment. This one was dark, the other light. But lightness and darkness followed one another more in an alternating sequence than in a relationship of origin and effect. This alternation was a sign that would be furnished to men, a sign according to which they could order their lives: their work and cessation, their activity and rest. The perfection of this ordering was destroyed by the darknesses of sin. But when the Son became man, he did not abolish creation's law of day and night. Instead, he simply led it beyond itself by bringing the light of God, so that, with it, he could fight against the darkness of hell; he could break through its night with the radiance of this light, not simply to chase darkness out of the world, but to fill it with a wealth of divine meaning.

He spoke about the night that was soon to come upon him and the disorientation it would bring. But suddenly, as if the passing time allotted for his work were too brief and the sequence of day and night too restricted for his activity, he invented something

new. He took upon himself the night of death, suffered through it and brought from it the dawning
of a new day of life. And the Creator answered him
from heaven by having the darkness of nature fall
over his death. The promise of the Spirit was already
manifest in this answer. Night breaks into day in order to announce the dawning of a new age; it will
be an age that bears the mark of the Son and that the
Father accepts in the Spirit of the dying Son. And
the accord between the Creator and the Redeemer
may extend so far that, in order to disseminate the
darkness of the Cross, and indeed the night in general, the Father had already secretly created out of
the Son's night. Out of the excess that lies in the
Son's surrender to the Father and to men.

Three nights are interconnected: the night of Creation, the night of sin, and the deepest of all nights,
the Father's abandonment of the Son while he, immersed in the world's darkness, carries the world's
sins into the realm of death. He does this in a way
that is manifest to the eyes of all; the apostles and
the women perceive it, and even the unbelievers notice it. And the Father watches over it from heaven
to see that the work be carried out all the way to
the end. It has lived from all time in the triune God
and now it also ought to come to life in men's faith.

When a believer begins to contemplate the Lord's
life, he will try to look upon it with his inner eyes, to
imagine scenes of the Lord's interactions with men,
of his preaching and miracles, in order to achieve a

fervent adoration; he will surrender himself to the Lord in order to be formed by him, to be transformed, and consigned to the Father's hands. In contemplative prayer, a part is always left to the one praying so that he may fashion it in freedom; and if the one praying is a beginner (but is anyone ever more than just a beginner?), he will prefer to choose images that are easy to imagine, words that have some connection with his daily life. For the most part, he will recoil in shyness from the mystery of the Cross, he will bring it into his prayer only surreptitiously and without letting it unfold, surrounding it with the words of a respect that does not seek to understand. When it comes close to him, he will hold his breath just like a diver. But the Lord has mercy on those who belong to him and finds ways to lead them even into the mystery of the night.

To be sure, he may not desecrate what belongs entirely to the Father; he cannot indiscriminately hand it over to those who do not understand it. But he is also not permitted to keep it entirely for himself, because it is the center of his gift of self. He therefore invites some people into his night, into this absence of vision and understanding, into a suffering that no longer has any human measure, because it receives its character entirely from the Lord. The state of the sufferer is at this point so immediately determined by his relationship to the Lord, that even the highest and rarest words prove to be incapable of expressing it. A John of the Cross, who was led into the mystery, speaks and sings of this, but he does so in the consciousness that he remains far behind the reality. What he says both is and is not at the same time: it is, because his piety expresses itself therein, because he attempts to describe, using the most profound comparisons he can find, what cannot be expressed, because he seeks in vain to bind and to unravel unspeakably intertwined experiences of fear, faith, abandonment and darkness. But the unraveling is fruitless, the binding even more so, because the unity lies in the Lord alone and is something inseparable from him, something he gives as his own possession. And the sharp edges of this unity do not let themselves be veiled, the best raiment tears like useless rags, the mystery bristles with jagged, hard and naked edges. It is just as useless to try to lay bare its essence; the human element, no matter how holy, clings to it; one cannot feel out the contours, or objectify them for contemplation.

No one is permitted to pray to receive the night, but every person ought to pray for the sake of the night. He ought to venture into the Lord's darkness, accompany the Lord along the way of the Passion, conceive and express prayers that proceed with him toward the Father. But for the Son, it remains a path of night, of being cast out into the unknown, of perfect alienation from self. If he appears once again among his own in the Resurrection, his face is still marked by the experience of the unfathomable depths. They do not recognize him; they think he is the gardener or a foreign traveler on the way to Emmaus. They have remained in their faith far behind the experience that he underwent in death. They do not have an inkling that there could be life again on the other side of this experience of death, a life out of death, eternal life. The night has marked him so deeply that none of them on their own can decipher the sign they see in his face.

But from this night comes the life of resurrection, from this night comes the Church, so tender and yet so hardy. Through the Church, the one who prays knows that this night is the most important of all, and that, even if he is not personally called to plunge into the night, he must nevertheless pray for its sake; for the Cross cannot be foreign to any prayer for the Church and for the Lord's work. The Christian cannot choose which Christian mysteries to deal with; he himself is chosen and brought into the whole, and the night, too, lies in this whole. The Lord indeed said "The poor you will always have among you", people who are in need of consolation, of words and works of corporal mercy, of charitable love. But this love at one point was fully immersed in the night. There it received a Christian stamp. There it took on the features of the One who entered the realm beyond seeing or understanding. And if we adore divine love and pray for love, then *this* love is the only love we can pray for, because this is the love that belongs to the Son, the love that radiates immediately from him. It pours forth most in the place where its flow seems weakest, it moves most in the place where everything seems stuck, it carries along and makes demands most in the place where the Son dies in the most extreme loneliness. If we turn our eyes away from the night, we no longer see the demands; we become lukewarm and our prayer becomes superficial and our word becomes empty and our silence emptier still.

One can raise the question of what contribution this contemplative involvement with the night makes to the real night in the Church. One who prays can offer only what he has: his poor daily life and its hidden mystery of grace. This mystery lies in him and above him as a radiant light, which he hopes to embody in his life through the power of love, of the Lord. Between the two stands something in the middle: the burning demand, which can never be dismissed, abandoned, or escaped, to bring about something of permanent value in our lives. It is not merely an ethical demand, which can be made intelligible, but rather one that rises out of the darkness that cannot be illuminated for reason, the darkness that allows nothing but a blind, groping advance and that communicates the intimation of a presence that does not show itself and nevertheless stands behind everything.

Christian existence, in this respect, has a certain

kinship with the night. The presence, in the silence
of which this existence plays itself out, and which is
the reason why it lays such a radical claim on man,
is the presence of the night itself and the hidden
presence of Christ in the night: as when a person
stands at night in a room, and one cannot see him,
but at most one hears him breathe. It is the same
presence, out of which the Son's answer to the Father originally rang; indeed, it is the point of origin of the mission, in which the Father, Son and
Spirit in unison decided on the Son's Incarnation;
in which day finally dawns for the sinner, in which
night finally falls for the Son, and both encounter
one another and interpenetrate one another in such
a pure way that it is impossible to determine where
the end or the beginning is, and only the long series
of the Lord's days on earth come into view. There
is therefore a kinship between all living faith and the
night, and the believer too, though he does not un-
dergo the night in an experiential way, can involve
himself with it in contemplation.

There is a contemplation of the night that takes
place in the day and on the basis of the "day". This
is the contemplation of the Lord's life, of his miracles and words, his challenges for me, his presence,
which takes hold of my entire person. A contemplation of the Mother's consent, her disposition, her
path. A contemplation of the Son's path, all the way
to the Passion, all the way to the dread he underwent

on the Mount of Olives. Here, the one who contemplates runs up against a limit: the mystery withdraws into the inaccessible solitude between the Father and the Son, and prayer is unable to reach any further, whether it itself remains in the day at this point or whether it enters with the Son into the night. But there can also be a prayer made out of the night, and in this case we have to speak of the inverse experience. The one who prays begins enveloped by the night, covered in its non-understandings and misunderstandings, among nothing but nameless things that lie beyond his ken, and he is cast out in infinite fatigue and sickness and endless despondency, in order to find his way back from the night to his own daily life. He is thrown out of the night *into the night*; in the night, he perceives at the same time a new night, which until now had escaped his notice: his participation in the Lord's night creates in him a sensorium for the Church's night, the night of those who suffer and of believers in general; a certain coldness and alienation, which comes from the Lord's night, accompanies him and can no longer be completely sent away. It is like a deposit that God has made in this man, so that he will not forget to be ready at any time and at the slightest hint to turn around and enter once again, to allow himself again to be shaken to the core of his being, in order better to be cast out of the night once again into the world.

And, to be sure, the Resurrection is a victory, but it is at the same time the emergence out of this night into the world that has no desire to understand. Once again, the Lord enters into his relationship, not only with the Mother, but also with the disciples, who constantly fail to understand and constantly must be converted anew. Of course, the Lord now carries the mark of the Resurrection, but the sign of the night remains, and at no time will the Mother forget how it looked beneath the Cross. And John will never recover from it; he is the witness, he knows what he saw. And the others know at least what they heard about it. All of them carry in themselves a vestige of this night. And the fact that the Lord then ascends into heaven and sends out the Spirit and makes the disciples into true apostles, who are permitted to die as martyrs in the manner established by God, does not free them from the fact that the Son died on the Cross for them, it does not free them from this night and from the contemplation of this night. They remain—and every believer and person at prayer remains—encompassed by the night, by a world that is not of this world, by a fulfillment that goes beyond any promise, by a mystery that does not belong to them, but to God alone.

Since the Son is both God and man at once, the contemplation of his essence and life can move in both spheres; but it must always pass from one over into the other. Neither sphere may be cut short on account of the other.

When the Son becomes man he inhabits a body that is exposed to the same dangers and accidents as is any other human body. But he remains God and retains the same vision of the Father and of the Spirit he had when he was only in heaven. The two spheres come together in him. He offers both to the one who contemplates: on the one hand, that which is nearest at hand and seems long familiar and trivial, and on the other, that which is furthest from him and is scarcely conceivable.

We see this clearest, perhaps, in suffering. Everyone is familiar with bodily pain; everyone has undergone the death of a loved one; everyone knows the limits of his own existence, not only in space and time, but also in what he is able to achieve and endure; everyone knows the limits of his spiritual vision. And yet the Lord's Cross contains fully impenetrable mysteries that lie far beyond these limits, mysteries that occur between God and God and can be truly understood only from within this relationship. Nevertheless, God reveals something of these mysteries so that prayer may not be abandoned to human limitations. Pain, wounds and death were for a long time things that belonged to human beings; there even existed among them the extreme poverty of Job, who owned nothing more than a sore-covered body. If the Son's body now hangs on the Cross, his suffering seems to be nothing but a new link in an immeasurable and long familiar chain. However, because the Son is God, all suffering receives a new value by virtue of the Cross. It is henceforward a com-passion, a suffering-with, a co-enduring of bodily and spiritual pain, indeed, a co-abandonment by God. The boundaries open up into one another. Whether one suffers much or little, he is allowed to stand in the light of the Cross, allowed to take a share of the burden that he does not see, does not know, does not understand, and in fact would not want to understand. Thus, the meaning of suffering flows into the meaning of the Cross.

This does not entitle human suffering to put on a haughty face, or become self-satisfied; it also does not lighten the burden. But it transforms pain in its innermost core. Pain receives a share in redemption. This may be a consolation to the sufferer, but it is in the first place a duty. And it is in any event an introduction into the Lord's prayer, into his openness to the Father. Perhaps the sufferer had previously preferred to be alone; he withdrew into himself, closed in upon himself; he bore the bitterness of suffering in solitude and was happy to see it abate. Now, his attitude toward suffering is no longer at his own disposal.

It may be that he has to be oppressed by some triviality and must find some extreme suffering bearable. The incongruence that comes to light remains a sign that the disciple is placed soul *and* body into God's service and has therefore surrendered the right to dispose over the relationship between the two. One person can suddenly, in the midst of the most acute pains, experience the seriousness of his mission as if for the first time, while another can have lived for a long time in his mission and only at a later time be retrieved from suffering. But since both possibilities come from the Lord, both of them—the active following *and* the passive having to suffer—must be formed by prayer. In suffering, prayer acquires the form of suffering; it is perhaps nothing more than a cry of suffering, a groan, a word that has dried to a trickle in the space of an hour, and yet God can invest this prayer with so much of the Spirit's power that it opens up new and unprecedented space for that contemplation and the emptiness of suffering is filled by the Lord, by his life, his teaching and his Church.

And if a sufferer happens to have little interior spiritual experience, he nevertheless knows that his suffering exists for the service of others, and that each member of the communion of saints can make use of it. He thus comes to understand somehow that his duty to the Lord follows a path that passes through the Church, and that in each personal vocation God always co-intends all of the others. Thus, the Church is joined together with the sufferer, and indeed already with every person at prayer, in a relationship in which they reciprocally affect one another, a relationship that can arise only from the Lord. The distribution of the graces of suffering lies in his hand; he makes use of them as he wishes; he can also change roles, now giving a person more suffering, and then reducing it again later, or giving something else or perhaps something completely the opposite. All of this is part of the same task, which fills the Christian's entire life, indeed, the entire duration of the Church.

As long as sin continues to exist in the world, the Lord will not cease his summons to suffer. He will demand more and more, with a mercilessness that arises from the mercilessness of his own suffering. He does not do so out of revenge or gloating [*schadenfreude*], still less in the manner of those who have undergone everything themselves and therefore accord themselves the right to require something similar of another, but simply because the state of the world authorizes him and compels him to do so, because the word that he gave to the Father wills to be honored in community with his brothers whom he came to lead home.

To contemplate means to watch with the eyes of prayer. To look upon the mysteries that Scripture reveals to us, and to see them as things and truths that a man can live and experience. Moreover, not to see them as faded perspectives from a time long past, but to see them in an alert and attentive way, in the awareness that the Son desires to encounter us in what we see as immediately as he did the people of that time: through his words, but no less through the works he performed, through the people who surrounded him, who believed in him, who witnessed his miracles, through his prayer and through his vision of the Father, through his suffering on the Cross in abandonment, between the two thieves. His words have lost nothing of their power, his works reach us over the passing of time.

His cry of abandonment pierces our ears in its nakedness and discloses itself to our contemplation in faith. It offers itself to anyone who would like to believe, and who hopes to receive from the Cross new nourishment for his faith. There is the nourishment of Flesh and Blood in the Eucharist, but there is also the nourishment that lies in contemplation. Food, in this case, means a new influx of living reality, being enriched through exchange with the Lord, being brought to give oneself to the Lord in his giving himself to us. To this food also belongs precisely the cry of abandonment. The Father listens to it because it carries the Son's sacrifice. But men need it no less; indeed, God needs it only for their sake. For this reason, the one who contemplates has the urgent duty to hear the cry, and, hearing it, to answer it. Each person knows that he is included in this cry, that the Lord is calling out for him, just as he calls out to the Father on his behalf. No matter on what level of faith a person happens to be, he can answer this cry. And he must answer it.

The first answer is simply the listening itself. A listening that does not stop up its ears, that is not simply escape and evasion, not simply hope that one will be able to interpret this call differently from the way it is meant. But rather one must listen to it in nakedness, in order to understand the naked Lord. In order to have nothing else in one's ears and in one's soul than this single call to the Father. One must listen to it so intently that, in listening, one begins to call out along with the Lord, in the loneliness of the Cross, for the one and only thing necessary: the Father. Everything else is excluded and set aside: the demand for consolation or insight or reason or vision. This is contemplation in nakedness, which wants nothing else but God.

After this, and completely secondarily, the one who prays will at some point learn what really is to become of him. The primary thing is that he gets an idea of what happens to the Lord. This is the law of contemplation, not merely the contemplation of the Cross, but of all contemplation of the Lord: that the one who prays become empty of himself in order to adapt himself to what the Lord is. In order with him and in him to say what he says, to attune his voice so closely to the Lord's that the Father can hear them as *one* voice. This unison is what first allows us to understand something like a putting on the mind of the Lord, a call, a mission, a genuine life of discipleship. Contemplation presupposes a dying to self: a dying to one's own will and to all of the gifts of understanding and seeing bestowed on man. To desire to exist, not in the I, but in the Thou; without restriction, without a measuring of distance, without a feeling of one's own unworthiness, and thus in the faith of a child who has been called and, through the call, has been drawn forward.

It is no game; it is no make-believe; rather, it is an integration that God himself has demanded: we have to contemplate the Lord with the Lord's own eyes. With the fullness of him who is the embodiment of the Gospel, we must contemplate every mystery of salvation history, surrender ourselves to it, recognize it as the highest reality, a reality that is so strong that this history has the power to bring all things under the influence of this newly dawning reality. Whoever looks upon the world's misery through the Cross, whoever draws closer to the suffering of the children of men through the Lord's suffering, is ready to arrange his contemplation in the proper way to experience the power of prayer, to receive the mysteries of the Lord's Incarnation and crucifixion; he is ready, moreover, to receive even the mysteries of the triune God as they have been revealed, and to be changed by them.

# 6. Awakening from the Night

A Christian who has begun to contemplate in most cases needs someone to instruct and guide him, or else he runs the danger of getting lost. It must be shown to him that he has to look away from himself, indeed, he has to forget himself and ought never to let his attention stray from his thoughts of God, not even for a moment. Contemplation is a vision that opens only to one who turns his gaze away from himself and toward God. The beginner will have a constant tendency to put himself, if not in the center, at least in a prominent place, and, since he is in this place, will not be able to refrain from constantly becoming part of the matter of contemplation himself. Whoever climbs a tree in order to pick cherries turns his entire attention to the fruit: he wants to secure as many as he can from the broadest area possible. He will of course attempt to find the correct place on the branch; but then he will not be constantly preoccupied with the position of his body, or with how risky the place he is sitting is. Instead, he will be focused on the harvest he takes in. And it will doubtless take more time in his first attempts than in his later ones to get into the correct position. The one who contemplates is in a similar situation. He must find as quickly as he can the position in which he forgets himself in order to be entirely taken up with the things belonging to God. And the great fruit will not be the result of a clever calculation, but rather of one's undivided attention, which does not allow itself to stray from whatever grace illuminates and offers.

When an experienced spiritual director teaches someone to pray, he gives him a few suggestions, like an orchardman who has been the one to do the harvesting, but now allows his son to climb the tree. He tells him to pay attention to this branch, and to stay clear of that one, because it is not sturdy. Afterward, when the harvest has been brought in, he can get a sense of whether his son did things correctly. Similarly, a director can discern to some extent from the account the novice gives whether he has gone about his contemplation in a correct manner, even though he cannot check on everything in detail. But he will also be able to draw certain conclusions regarding his contemplation in addition from the way the novice behaves in other areas of his life.

Nevertheless, there will always be something that lies beyond his oversight: namely, that which God always gives to the individual alone. There remains an innermost sphere, which one cannot describe as "private" because it remains open to the Church, but which forms God's reservoir—perhaps for particular instructions or tasks in his mission; perhaps, by contrast, for the sake of allowing this individual to participate in a community of contemplatives that remains unknown to him, and this can be a gift of the night.

The Church's guidance teaches one to turn away from oneself; it leads to a sort of aptitude test for the possible gift of an experience of the night. Normally, the beginning of this experience presupposes an inclusive consent to the Church's guidance, indeed, an inclusive readiness in both the director and the novice to grant validity to God's will in all of its unconditionality and to accept it. And it is also proper for the director discreetly to test and to introduce a certain delay in order to be certain that the path taken truly corresponds to God's will. It is proper for the director to come to a sort of agreement with God, similar in a sense to the way in which both one's father *and* mother must agree that the child go to this particular school or study for this particular profession. And now something happens in that hidden area, which the director is no longer able to follow directly, although he does not cease sharing in it in an indirect way. He gives the instruction: surrender everything, give yourself away entirely. And he can no longer follow the flight of the balloon. He has placed the person praying into

God's hands, he can no longer record the details of what is happening before him. Thus, in the contemplator's act of surrender there is also the director's act of surrender, and behind this, there is that of the Church. The director stands there in readiness; one can go to him; but at the same time he is absent, because he must withdraw before God.

If God sends the night to the person praying, he is generally not spared from sharing everyday life with other people. He will do so in a somewhat routine manner or even in indifference, accompanied by a mild resistance. He is like one who is capable of taking only particular steps, because a fence or something like a cord is preventing him from engaging in movements that would otherwise be possible without effort. Not merely his prayer, but the whole of his efforts and his disposition are embraced within the Cross and its night. And he must undertake his everyday life from out of this night, he must at the same time discover new forms of prayer and new methods of contemplation, he must learn how to gain insight into new aspects of the Lord's suffering. He will be led to this insight, but he must also make a certain contribution himself.

It is possible that this inner instruction be connected to things that he had previously experienced as personal affronts or to things that other people, whom he only fleetingly knows, have undergone. Or perhaps to things that have remained unclear to him until now, maybe because he hesitated, interiorly, to look at them, to retain them, and to extract a meaning from them. If God shows himself in the night, he clears space with the most unexpected and apparently most out-of-the-way things; he does not desire to reveal himself anew merely in the withdrawal that the night represents, but he desires to create new air and to carry out a sort of general confession in the life of the person contemplating: confession not merely as an avowal, but above all as a profound insight into and weighing of sin. In this respect, things may be at issue which have been known, discussed, suffered through, and even absolved and forgotten a long time ago in a different context, but which must now be lived through once again in a completely different way, without the light of a felt presence and without consolation.

Undergoing this experience becomes a precondition for awakening out of the night. Once it comes to an end, then the light can, with the force of a resurrection, flow into the person praying. Then, the person no longer recognizes himself; he no longer understands what went before, but he nevertheless carries within himself this lived experience, which he is no longer permitted to forget apart from a particular task given by God. He has tasted something of the Son's loneliness on the Cross—a drop, not the whole. And this experience brought to life a reverence in him that rules out any confusion between him and the Lord, between his tiny experience and the enormous depth of what the Lord underwent. He will henceforward lose any desire to use the words "Cross" and "Passion" lightly. He will no longer inflate his own worries, he will no longer casually draw a connection between his painful experiences and difficulties and the Lord's suffering. Instead, he will show a modesty that reserves grand words for what the Lord has borne.

He will be like a convalescent, to whom life is again returning—a life, however, that also promises more responsibilities because of the ever-living experience. There are people who have never undergone an operation and who speak from start to finish about the horror of being sick and of surgery, and about its residual pains. But if they happen to experience themselves even a glimmer of such things, they nearly pass out at the mere mention of some technical terms connected with surgery. Something of this "holy horror" remains in the convalescent and causes him above all to remain conscious of his infinite distance from the Lord's suffering. Thus, he lives in a wholly new reverence, which is connected with gratitude and childlike surrender. His surrender is thus transformed, so that he has now come to understand the Lord's surrender, but he has also experienced how little disposal and management a believer has over his own surrender. He knows that he must throw himself into it, and then he must attempt to allow what is in itself the most extreme to happen to him. He will then eliminate the words "up to this point (and no further)" from his vocabulary. Since he has learned that the limits of his capacity to suffer do not lie where he thought they did, he will give up altogether talking about limits. And everything in life will take on a new value and will in a new way lose value. The new value will lie in the fact that he is able to give to the Lord more from what is offered to him and to make it useful to him, and many things, to which he had been attached, he now has less trouble giving up, because they show themselves to be without value in comparison with the truly valuable.

But the night can recur, and then every departure from the night is a new awakening. World and surroundings and occupations and to a certain extent faith itself are given as a new gift. And to be sure this does not happen merely after a genuine night which, like the night experienced by John of the Cross, fills the entire depths of the soul, but also after a contemplation of the night, either one that has been laid upon a person as a task or one that is freely chosen, which was prayed through in a serious way, and in which the Passion opened itself up in its uniqueness and in its sudden and irrevocable character. In this case, for the duration of the night, there is no possibility of shielding oneself or finding one's way back, and even the thought of such things does not offer itself to the spirit. Such a thought would be a straying thought, a thought of resistance and disobedience, even if it is looking out for a way to lighten the experience. The Son, who was constantly aware ahead of time that he would have to suffer nevertheless left the hour to the Father so completely that it suddenly crashed over him with a violence, with an ultimate force. He did not prepare himself for this hour; he did not attempt to bear more and more on the way to the Cross, like a wonder-worker who can unfold his powers further and further, to the amazement of those around him. If he had done so, he would have deferred the hour of his death, and it would thus no longer have been the Father's hour.

The Cross is a unique event. Everything the Lord has shared about the Cross with those who followed him through the ages arises from its uniqueness. They can therefore never add their own hours of suffering to it in such a way that the addition of all these hours could somehow be compared with the Lord's hour. For it is not the duration of worldly time that provides the measure here, but rather its depth and intensity, and the Passion of the God-man brooks no comparison in this regard.

Nevertheless, the Lord's invitation to participate in his night is total and genuine. He does not hide anything from those who are invited; it is just that they lack the strength, in prayer, in letting-be and in capacity to bear as much as he offers to them. They remain at a distance, even if they do not feel the distance, because their tiny vessel is already so full, because they have been taken up into something greater and they can perceive no empty place in their consciousness. What they experience is the fact that they have entered into something that has no limits, something that has taken their own limitations into itself in order to free them from them—through a process that remains hidden from them.

A person who loves with the ultimate and most fulfilling love can still harbor doubts whether his love could not in fact be more ardent, more single-hearted, or could make itself more useful. Shouldn't he show more to the beloved; shouldn't he not only give more, but also possess more for his sake and hold itself more ready; shouldn't he thus be far more strongly possessed by love? But the hold that the night of suffering has on the person praying has a harshness that does not allow any such reflections. The suffering is just what it is, neither more nor less. This 'just' is so definitive, that all discussion is impertinent. Nevertheless this 'just' has its extension, indeed, it has its center, in the Lord; it remains in him as his property, and whatever aspect of it he shows to the person praying is at the same time merely an aspect of his revelation and expropriation, which is received in conformity to his will. This conformity is something the Lord himself brings about. Whatever might be given this name in man remains something that belongs to the Lord. "I live, not I, but Christ lives in me": St. Paul's expression receives here a fulfillment brought about by the Lord himself.

When the believer eventually has to leave the night behind, then even this departure once again corresponds to a demand. This demand is connected with a second one: to make something out of the night that has been experienced. The response to God cannot be abruptly broken off, as if there were now nothing more to derive from this relationship of suffering to the Lord. The new day that dawns must be stamped by the night that is passing away. And this demand is new each time. It is never something to which one grows accustomed. The new day is as fresh as the Resurrection, and its entire novelty must be tasted by a wholly fresh soul. And as much as joy may predominate in this experience, it is nevertheless the carrying out of a task and not at all an indulgent letting-oneself-go. That the joy corresponds to the night that has been weathered just as the Resurrection corresponds to the Crucifixion is something that also belongs to the Lord's demand. Thus, a doctor who has just undergone a serious illness attempts to incorporate some of the fruit of his own experience into his subsequent activity. He does not reflect on past suffering in order to take delight in the fact that he survived it, but in order to gain and hold fast to something for the sake of his task.

But there is not only the awakening into the full light of day; there is also a certain awakening that occurs within the night itself. Thus, the night can be ordained for an entire period of time (for example, Lent), and within this period there can be moments of the most intense and passive night alongside moments that turn somewhat toward day, in which a person must so to speak take in the harvest of the experience of night. In the thick of the night, only a minimum of active contribution is possible in contemplation. On the one hand, this is because the person praying has to be much more discrete, and must stick much more closely to what is given; moreover the angst that always hangs over the night prevents free discretion in the matter of contemplation. On the other hand, this is because the Gospel's human words and human portrayal open up much more quickly into the unknowable divine. Everything is much more immediately revealed and examined by God, and the fruit, which is indeed in some sense always at hand, remains invisible to the one contemplating.

Nevertheless, there are also contemplations of the night in which the person is left a certain freedom of movement; the fact that things remain veiled does not mean that they are unclear; only rarely are the contemplations of the night sheer, dumb suffering, without a face. It is just that the one contemplating remains more still than usual; he does not dare to ask when there is something he does not understand, he does not take up any theme that has not been assigned to him; above all, he lets happen what must happen: for the most part, something apocalyptic is connected with the contemplations of the night, and therefore a person often must change place for their sake, they require a level different from that of ordinary contemplation.

Finally, in a period of night, there is also a certain contemplation of day, in which the person praying has even greater freedom of movement. If he happens to be required by his rule to observe a daily hour of contemplation, then today he will reconnect with the contemplations of the previous days —even when these were explicitly contemplations of the night. He will not be permitted to engage in his own activities until the entire period of the night has passed, but to the extent that room has been given to him for it (and it may in fact be very little room), he will sow and reap and maintain the flowing rhythm of prayer. He will let the effects of prayer work their way into him, he will expose one side or another of his soul to suffering with full awareness, in order to be purified, or merely in order to leave the choice of what is to be purified to the suffering, and he will hand over his whole self, his calling, and his mission, to the night. He will give up trying to figure out many points, and to determine particular details about the effects of suffering and its fruits, but will instead wait and give thanks.

But the fruit of this fruit, the final result, is something he will always have to ascertain, in order to incorporate it into his Christian mission, so that he can use it for particular tasks in his life and also for later times and to keep open other and different spiritual spaces, in which the memory of this experience will prove necessary for him. This result can remain alive in him as one of God's most hidden and perhaps never fully articulated demands, a demand that nevertheless must be heard, a demand that asserts its claim. One may also be called upon to put the experience into words and to allow it to turn into corresponding deeds, which show the Lord he did not make the gift of suffering in vain. If the mission of the person praying is an active one, then he will have to respond through actions. If it is a mission of contemplation and pure prayer, then he will have to allow his prayer ever anew to be reinvigorated by suffering and by God's weighing of it.

# 7. Drawing Near

The Son became man in order, through his death and Resurrection, to lead us into the eternal life of the triune God. In this respect the faith that has been given to us is, already in this world, an invitation to eternal life. The more a person believes, the more profoundly will this invitation take hold of him. Through prayer and contemplation, he will become capable of an ever deeper grasp of God's revelation in his Son. This revelation takes him into itself, just as he is, with all of his capacities and talents, and nothing that is worthwhile in him will be rejected. He enters into faith as a whole, and it is as a whole that he must concern himself with the word of revelation.

This means first of all reading holy Scripture and receiving God's word, just as it presents itself, with the intention of offering it a dwelling place in which it can take effect in him even beyond the time set aside for reading. But one cannot encounter the word merely through reading; rather, the reading will drive a person to prayer. This prayer will initially be a prayer of joyful thanksgiving for the riches that have been received; it will be poor in content, something like a series of exclamation points that are meant to indicate grateful joy, and sometimes also, perhaps, the pain of one's own unworthiness. If the reading and prayer resonate with one another, it will gradually become clear to the believer that they belong together, that the word itself contains the task of forming a unity out of the two: this is ultimately what gives rise to contemplation in the usual sense. The object of contemplation is the incarnate Word in its entire fullness, which includes both its form as ecclesial doctrine and also its opening up into eternal life. The Word's invitation to follow him into eternal life does not remain distant and unintelligible, but contains within itself a task: namely, to understand.

In order to understand it, the believer must draw near to the Lord in contemplation: he must make the Lord the center of his own thought and desire; he must follow in the Lord's footsteps, one after the other, attempting to understand what it is the Lord is undertaking or leaving aside, what it is he is saying and why he is saying it. He must see the Lord not merely in an isolated divinity (which always remains in some sense abstract), but also in his relationship to his mother, to his disciples, and to everyone and everything around him. He must see him as the one who fulfills the Old Covenant, which gives the person praying the opportunity to include in his contemplation even the figures and words of

the Old Testament in their relationship to the incarnate Word. Finally, he must see the Son always
within his exchange of life and love with the Father
in the Holy Spirit.

The purpose of this prayerful contemplation is to
acquire an inner understanding of the Word, and
if possible to read off his desires from his eyes, to
achieve insight into his demands, even the ones that
he does not explicitly formulate; why he speaks here,
and remains silent there, why he comes forward this
time, and another time disappears into the crowd.
Why he prays in solitude, hidden from all, and once
again in public in front of his disciples. What profound consistency there is in all of these modes of
relationship.

When someone learns about the striking and apparently meaningful things another person has said
or done, he harbors a desire to get to know this
person. He would like somehow to be able to catch
sight of the missing pieces in the fragmentary expressions that would bring the wholeness that lies
behind them into view. And if he knew, moreover,
that this person harbored a love for him, and had
been intending for a long time to extend to him an
invitation, then he would feel even more strongly
moved by the little that he knows and would burn
with a desire, finally, to meet the one that he has
admired. No amount of instruction from him would
be enough to give him the most complete picture

possible. Now, every believer knows that the Lord
loves him and invites him, that the Lord has questions to pose to him and waits anxiously for answers,
and that the Lord is ready to help him and to embrace him within his creative life. The believer even
knows that this invitation is to lead him to the eternal vision of the triune God. He was given his life in
order to prepare for this vision, and becoming ready
for it is not something he must accomplish on his
own; the Lord comes to help him and teaches him
through Scripture and through the Church's word,
and his instructions are wholly understandable. And
man's responses also possess full validity, no matter how imperfect they happen to come out. Man
knows what he must say, even if he cannot manage
a pure assent.

Moreover, the Lord gives himself to the believer
in the sacraments, especially in the Eucharist; though
not perceivable by the senses, he can be grasped in
faith. The forms of bread and wine do not represent limitations either to his presence in this place
or to his effect at a particular time: the Eucharist
is a radiant, self-giving and comprehensive presence.
Scripture's word and the sacrament converge with
one another; every word that the person praying
contemplates and receives places him immediately
and personally in the presence of the Lord, which
is given to him in the sacrament. He can build
his entire contemplation around the center of the

eucharistic miracle, around the simultaneously sacramental and spiritual reception of the Father's eternal Word with all that the person praying can awaken in himself in faithful readiness and understanding. Eucharist and contemplation interpenetrate one another in a fruitful act, whose beneficiary is the believer. This act overflows its borders: whoever truly believes cannot but desire to share apostolically what he has received; he *must* do so, in order to remain obedient to the task of faith. Obedience is therefore itself a form of drawing near. And obedience has an inner connection with poverty and virginity: the Lord's counsels, and their spirit—borne of faith, hope and love and included within the circle they form—belong to the act of drawing near, which gives a powerful boost to our understanding of the Lord.

Our drawing near to the Lord is based entirely on his drawing near to us. He embraces the whole of the law for us in the two commandments to love God and to love our neighbor, and this commandment is now both at the same time: an expression of his own attitude, in which he draws near to us sinners as the Holy One, and the expression of the task he gives to us, in which we are able to draw near to him and find him. He stands in the center of this commandment: insofar as he gives us this commandment to keep, he thus gives us himself.

When we carry out this commandment, we catch a glimpse of him; to fulfill it means, in his Spirit, to draw near both to the Father and to our fellow men. Our neighbor is imperfect; in fact, he is a sinner. We must therefore learn to look on him with the Lord's eyes of love, and we will be able to love him in truth only by virtue of the Lord's love. But if we, moreover, make the human life that the Lord lived among us the object of our contemplation, then we will learn to recognize his closeness to us in all of its love-filled radiance. This is how God approaches us who are sinners! And his commandment of love is the means that he gives to us to draw near to the one who draws near to us. In contemplation itself, we suddenly see sparks shoot up out of his earthly existence, which approaches us and enters into the prayer with which we approach him, and both of these are the same reality, the same love that God has given to us. It is to be sure an active love, love as charity for our brother, but it is also and to the same extent a contemplative love, which is given to us here just as the act of the Incarnation of God's love remains an after-effect of his heavenly love that contemplates the world.

We, to whom the commandment of love has been given, experience the inner effectiveness of this gift. We do not need constantly and anxiously to verify what effects this Christian love has had, which we have attempted to exemplify. Instead, we should be reassured in faith that the explosion of this love has

occurred in us, there where the Lord's love has con-
descended to include us in its work.

Whoever experiences this in some way, moreover,
does not shrink from becoming a contemplative in
the stricter sense. Like Elijah, he allows himself to be
led into solitude and does not fret over food or sustenance. The fact that Elijah was fed by ravens was a
sign; whoever withdraws for the sake of contemplation will be fed by God's word itself. And the food,
the word that the person praying incorporates into
the core of his being will become for him a supreme
intimacy, the very presence of the Lord in him, who
does not live in him like a foreign body, but like self-
giving and self-communicating love, which through
this giving of itself builds the person praying up from
the inside.

Thus, the word becomes at once food and life, in
order to serve divine love. As self-giving word, it
is the servant of love, and as such wishes to return
to the source of love. It is thus a circling word for
circling love. The Son shows us this circle in which
he comes from the Father and returns to the Father,
and thus draws near to sinners and non-believers and
takes hold of those who have achieved faith and provides them with food and life.

There is a worldly description of the human being,
his essence and manifestations, which is called sci-
entific in the exact sense. And it is indeed exact,
within its own realm, even though in every human

being, both in his supernatural calling and mission, there lies a mystery that escapes all earthly science. But prayerful contemplation can never be for us "exact", because "exactness" remains enclosed within the Lord. We contemplate as precisely as we are able; but we cannot and ought not to contemplate in an "exact" sense, because we must contemplate at a distance from ourselves, and thus there is always something of ourselves that we must disregard. We turn our glance away from that within us which wants less, which loves less; we renounce these things in order to cultivate perfect love and desire. And this renunciation ought to be so complete that we no longer know anything about it; that it belongs to the "freely given grace" and thus enables us to experience something of true love: to contemplate, in true love, what true love is. Then something happens to us that carries us into the circling motion of the Son's love as it travels from the Father and returns to him, brings us in a sense to the center, which cannot be any more precisely defined but is nevertheless absolutely true.

In this way, genuine intimacy in life becomes possible. Prayer is fostered by the commandment of love and nourished by the Eucharist. It had its full resonance in every word that the Lord spoke on earth, and all the words gathered together into a unity give us some idea of the overwhelming power of the primal, eternal tone that is the Word itself. This primal

Word is ineffable. But when the Son dwells among men, he does not want them to die or become paralyzed through fear; they ought to receive his word and carry it out and grasp the meaning and goal of his coming and staying and going away again. This is why he explains himself through a variety of words. Every person receives his invitation, everyone receives his place at the banquet, everyone receives his own mission, and thus everyone is permitted to live in love in such a way that he can make his own contribution to its work.

In creating man, God gave him speech, in order that he might make himself understandable to his brother, but also that he might cultivate a relationship and a spiritual exchange with his Creator. Both God and creation ought to find their expression in the word. And since the Father created man in view of the Son and made him a gift to the Son, he implanted in man a reflection of the word-character of the Son. Man is gifted with a word that belongs to the Father. And this word is not merely lent to him; instead, though it continues to belong to the Father, it passes over into man's possession. And this occurs in a drawing near to the Son's existence on earth, the Son who possessed the vision of the Father and acted as the Father's word in the world.

Having been gifted with speech, believers thus possess in word what pertains to the Father. They articulate it. But in this case it is no longer they who have mastery over the word; rather, the word governs them and elevates them. By the power of the word, they are moved toward the Father. They are not permitted to misappropriate this word; they are not permitted to utter it gratuitously and thanklessly. When they form it in their mouths, they give answer to the triune God's address to them and commandment to them with their own word: they are taken up into the most complete responsibility. This responsibility is so vast that it surpasses them, and this transcendence expresses the Son's character as the ever-greater, which becomes one of the fundamental characteristics of all things Christian. This does not correspond to a closed circle, a form or figure that would correspond to man's finite nature. Instead, it bears the traces of God's Incarnation.

The believer's Christian response is concrete, just like the Incarnation of God's Word in our midst. It is not a theory, it is not a question of good intentions, it is not a philosophy; rather, it is a graced participation in the reality of the triune God. The believer's word of prayer is as genuine as Jesus Christ's flesh and blood is genuine. Indeed, the word of the believing Church effects the presence of this Flesh and Blood in every holy Mass. The Church's word penetrates through the clouds and is heard and accepted by the Father, and the Father sends his Son to her for this reason. The Father recognizes this word as his own. Every Christian word of prayer, every Christian word uttered in faith and in responsibility, possesses something of this force, which penetrates to the Father. Words spoken gratuitously, on the other hand, words without significance or reality, even lofty words that have no relationship to the incarnate Son, do not penetrate to God. The language that a Christian has to speak is outlined for him by the Word of God. Even when he is silent, his silence must correspond to the Lord. And both of these, the speaking and the remaining silent, take their origin from the contemplation of the Lord's speaking and remaining silent, and from the carrying out of both. The believer contemplates in silence —which means that he listens—and in speech, that is, using the Son's word. Contemplation, from this perspective, is an expression of an answering responsibility to the word, and is given to the Christian by God, so that his word may be gathered up in contemplation, that its fullness may be assured, and that it may acquire the concreteness it is meant to possess.

Thus, the Christian inserts himself into the Word, and he is formed [*eingefügt*] into a person who makes himself available [*zum Verfügten*]. Into a person who offers himself to God, who draws near to God, who holds himself constantly ready for whatever task God wishes to give him. He thus resembles the incarnate Son, insofar as he does not live for himself but rather in surrender to his task, which is nourished through contemplation of the Father. No matter what shape a Christian life may have outwardly, the hour of contemplation is the hour of fructification. The mind opens itself to receive, the heart widens into a receptive vessel. The whole man is willing to adapt himself to the ever-greater character of divine truth.

This does not mean that man will be aware of the fullness that he receives in faith. It also does not mean that the word encounters him at every occasion like something unknown and never-before-seen that has fallen from heaven. He simply receives the word in the humble knowledge that even the incarnate Son did not know the Father's hour (Mk 13:32), but nevertheless experienced in various ways a veiling, disquiet, and anxiety in relation to the Father (Heb 2:18; 5:7–9). And that the personal destiny that is granted to the believer will prove to be to the very end a sign and indication of the Son's destiny. Nothing more. Even the saint never becomes simply a perfect human being. He becomes a man who lives on the basis of God's perfection, as one whose highest hope is to persist in the distance from God that has been established for him—precisely in this distance: without allowing himself to stray, to set up his own borders and outlines, or even to measure this distance.

If the Son shows himself as the Father's Word, then his word conveys a meaning: it is an expression of the Father's will. But it also accomplishes this will: his coming and his going reveal nothing other than the Father's will. And his expressions give evidence for the fact that he himself is the one expressed, that he brings about a unity between his human will and the Father's will with the whole of his being, and that he allows this unity to become real at every moment. His being among us is therefore to the same extent act, and his act, his work among us, is to the same extent being.

If he entrusts himself to us, then we must also, for our part, create a unity between the expressed word, which he is, and our own attitude; not merely for the brief duration of contemplation, but throughout the entire day.

As Christians, we express a word that has been lent to us, which demands nothing else but that we allow it to become our word and to express our own inner attitude. That we allow this word to have an inward effect on us, insofar as it determines our mental and spiritual attitude in prayer, but also for it to have an outward effect, by means of the things we do in harmony with it. If we contemplate, then the things of God stand open before our eyes for the space of a quiet moment, which has been set aside especially for this vision, in an appropriate space and in a particular state of mind. Then it may perhaps not seem so difficult for us to see God's truths as they come forward to meet us out of holy Scripture, and even to place the things of our everyday life into this higher light, and to recognize the everyday tasks that arise from this. Once we return to our world of work, however, we must preserve the same spirit: persisting in this intimacy with the Lord, which was given to us in contemplation, in the spirit of prayer, and mindfully carrying the Lord, as God's word, so that he can take effect within us. We must avoid becoming a constant obstacle to him, which he first must tediously clear away in order that we might be able to see and hear again; we must not become an impediment by constantly planning and pursuing something other than the task he has laid before us.

In the Son's human life there lies an inexhaustible model for everything, even for the most difficult of human situations. He offers himself to our contemplation as a resource, which does not only suffice for this single hour, but which can superabundantly fulfill the whole of our existence. This lies in the word's power to radiate, which is a power that consists entirely of love, in the exemplarity of its surrender, which will never be rescinded. It is thus enough that we turn our glance ever anew back to the Lord over the course of our day's work, in order to become aware of it and to turn back to the center of love. In this respect, we are like the pupil for whom the teacher has written out the first letters and who imitates them, with his eyes constantly on the model, however perfectly or imperfectly as he may manage to copy them. Contemplation remains present in the day's work. Every person who attempts to contemplate in earnest knows from experience how easy it is to slip away from the world of contemplation if one does not concern oneself with this presence, or if a few words or images from the morning prayer do not accompany one throughout the day.

The fact that something abides with us is part of prayer's closeness. The presence that was achieved in prayer has to be something that can be reproduced, at least in certain moments, when we are faced with the necessity of restoring to order something that has fallen out of place, into error, or has become alienated. The Son, who possessed the vision of the Father while he was on earth, has given us something of this vision in our contemplation of faith, so that we too can reap its fruitfulness for the sake of our earthly life. Just as the Son persists in vision, so too must we remain in the spirit of prayer. For the duration of our life, there will be nothing that brings us closer to God than prayer, which is fashioned out of God's own Word.

# 8. Images of the World

The things of this world, which God created, stand before him with their own form and truth. He knows them; he knows everything that concerns them. And his knowledge is not restricted to their present state; rather, he also knows what they were and what they will be. And he created them altogether in view of the Son. The "work" that he invested in them in creation will find its "reward" in the Son. He sees in them what they ought to become; he sees this in the Son himself, who will fulfill in himself all things in heaven and on earth. And thus things do not possess their truth merely in the fact that they correspond to the Creator's intention, but also in the fact that they represent for the Father countless points of access to the Son.

We experience things by means of images. They are, for us, a small snapshot of reality; we know the past only in a deficient way, and we are generally ignorant about the future; moreover the present moment is temporally and spatially limited. And as often as one thing turns itself to face us, another remains hidden. Images are fragmentary. If we had the power to love the Son so much that we carried him in ourselves in a living way, then he would enable us to have a better insight into the intimate connections within the world of images. We would then receive the capacity to see the completion that lies in the Son and that the Son grants to them. Contemplated from this perspective, they would become much more meaningful for us. We would see them within the relationship that discloses their ultimate truth, namely, the Father's relationship to the Son, the relationship that elevates and transforms things through the Son.

And the images are not only created things. They are also ideas, imaginings, experiences, moods, and desires—in short, everything that concerns us as human beings in any way. Whether my personal experiences are also accessible to others or not, whether they have their basis in Christian faith or not, or in certain previous life experiences, such as my education, or relationships, is for the moment irrelevant. The image of the world is there, and it wishes to be seen and understood just as it is. If we are people who pray, however, then we know that this image yields its definitive meaning in contemplation. Contemplation and prayer are for us always the way to ascertain God's truth and will. And this is not only in relation to God's heavenly mysteries, which were opened to us in revelation, but just as much in relation to the truth of his creation, which is ordered to the Son. The Son has always been in our midst and has already begun to bring about the recapitulation of all things in heaven and on earth. For the person praying, these things can be understood as preparations for his coming, as signs of his dwelling among us, as confirmations of the Passion he suffered, as ever-living recollections of his earthly existence, as means of the work on earth he continues to do from heaven. Thus, the world of prayer becomes a rich, variegated world full of images through the inclusion of things, a world that is at once infinite and finite, because the finite images find their spiritual place in the infinite and eternal image of God.

There are many things in our everyday lives on earth that we can make into signs of our faith through proper use. There are many things that are in our possession but which we can offer to God. And his response to our offer can take many forms: it can be that the Lord desires to take the thing for his own use, or that it can be useful for the Church, or that the person praying ought to keep it at his own disposal. But if the motive was genuine and the disposition pure, whatever the response is, it brings to light something positive, namely, a path to the Lord. Often we ourselves make a decision, but it ends in failure, because the Lord wishes to see it replaced by another order. This order thus becomes the true one, and it holds at the same time the value of his choice and the valuelessness of our own. This value-lessness does not need to be something merely neg-ative; it can also serve as a preparatory stage or as an occasion that later puts us in a position to renounce something, to lose something, or to allow it to be stolen from us by God's own hand.

The images are so numerous, it is impossible to survey them all. But we know that, in this fullness, the Father has already created them from the begin-ning in view of the Son. We ourselves belong to those things created with a view to the Son, but, as spiritual creatures with understanding, we have re-ceived a relationship to all these things through the Father's Word. This includes the things that have passed away, and also things that lie beyond the reach of our senses, in heaven, in the depths of the sea, or in the bosom of the earth: they are all, with all their mystery, ordered with us to the Son.

Other people and other ages experience different images; what is distant to us is near for them. But these distant perspectives are not foreign and without significance for us. They represent the world-images of our brothers in the Lord; these images are the ba-sis for their personalities and are for them pointers to God. They reveal to us something of the Church's mind and of her Communion of Saints. Just as all prayers enter individually into the Church's treasury, all the irreplaceable standpoints and perspectives of the individual people who pray are preserved. There remains the mystery that God shares with an individual, the stamp that God gives to him, the face that the person turns to God and in which God truly and uniquely knows the individual. For God does not view the person as a sum of characteristics, which others may also happen to have; he does not measure his sacrifice according to categories or place his prayers on a scale. He encounters each individual in just as personal a manner as he foresaw, affirmed and created him. The dignity of each person finds its reflection in the uniqueness of his world and in the images this world presents to him, and the person praying ought to remain conscious of their worth and value before God.

When we contemplate the Son on earth, we know that even his mind was surrounded by images. Many of these are so full of mystery that they remain for us completely abstract; other images form his daily experience, just as they form ours. A bench, a table, a place of rest, a meal. A conversation, a prayer. A vision of the Father. All of this is reality for him, and constitutes his human life. We can and should make all of this present to ourselves in our contemplation of the Son's life, in order to have his living figure before our eyes. Otherwise, we would run the danger of seeing him as altogether without relation in the world, and thus we would diminish his love in our representation; we would trivialize his sacrifice; we would sublimate his suffering, and allow even the Lord himself to become thin, distant, unreal and finally trite and sentimental, to the point that we forget his entire mission and retain from him in a certain sense nothing more than an inaccessible and unintelligible conversation with the Father. All the Lord's words were truly spoken, they came forth from a genuine human mouth, expressed with an audible voice, heard by ears of flesh and understood and answered in one way or another by concrete people. It is good that we know this not only from Jesus' words, but from the other things in his life that seem less lofty to us or closer to our own everyday lives. For our contemplation ought not to fly off into the clouds; it ought to be modeled on the reality as closely as possible. In this case, it is guaranteed to become fruitful in our lives.

Man stands in the world with a limited body whose movements in space are also limited. He has thoughts that roam much more broadly, and whose scope it is difficult to determine; nevertheless, one can say with certainty that even these are finite in content and extension. Whatever thoughts, hopes and plans a person wishes to call his own, and even whatever real things surround him with their hard contours, precisely the finitude of all these things shows that he cannot possess them forever; precisely in possessing them, man is constantly called to the possibility that he might have to renounce them or lose them.

The believer possesses things in one sense less and in another sense more than another person: less, because he has a deeper grasp of their ephemeral character; he does not need to think about the experience of another's death or about his own death, which he knows he will one day face; these things are familiar to him already by virtue of faith. The more alive his knowledge of eternal life is, the more concrete will be his knowledge of the passing away of time, of the course it follows into eternity. And on the other hand things belong to him more than to others: because he knows that they are ordered to Christ, because as a person who knows, he participates in the promises that include the entire world in the hope for eternal life.

He also knows that he must use things in a proper way. For this reason, he must look at them in the right way; he must deal with them with care, always keeping their ultimate purpose in view. They are reminders, because they all carry within them their Father's idea. They are signs marking out the way to him, because they point to the Son. In order to use them properly, the believer must order himself in relation to his faith. He will thus keep his eyes on two things: the joy that the Creator wishes to prepare for him through things, and the joy that will thus be set free for the Son. All things and their images have an inner core of joy. Because God, in creating the world, wanted so much to implant in man the joy he intended for him, he graced the images of things with beauty; and if this beauty was not perfectly perceptible in the manifestation of things, it nevertheless lies in the intention that the Creator ultimately carried out: even the most inconspicuous thing is beautiful because of its divine purpose.

To be sure, no beauty needs to be drawn from what is tasteless and kitschy; but Christians should still always strive in constantly renewed activity to make the beauty of the final end radiate in them and to be able to stimulate a pure joy in the Church's art, which was intended to glorify the Son and was offered up to him. The image of the divine ought to be genuinely beautiful, so that the adoration to which it gives rise can be genuine adoration, and the intention that lies behind the image may be the strong and true intention of love, which fits into the Creator's vast and objective loving intention to lead the things of the world to the Son.

Things glide at the same time along a moving path that travels from the Creator to the Redeemer and the Perfector of the world. Man is permitted to enter into this path and make his own contribution: to allow himself to be enriched by it as he travels it insofar as he, in turn, enriches the path through his own gift. He is permitted to use a thing in such a way and to a certain extent possess it in such a way that the one who will ultimately possess it, the Son, can recognize the imprint that the person has left on it. The things that are handed into the Son's charge rest in God's reality. The physical eye sees their image; but for the spirit they are even more visible; man on earth deals with their earthly manifestation, but faith and hope grasps them at a deeper level. The images move in time, but even this movement speaks to man of eternity. The ephemeral is so ephemeral only because it is a reflection of eternity. Form is so fragile because it strives after eternity, the limits are so hard because they stand over against the limitless. Whoever uses words like "everlasting", "eternal", or "limitless", already knows something of God. Indeed, more than that: he knows that God has given something to his created image during his journey, that God has breathed something everlasting into the ephemeral form. And thus the image acquires an inner relation to the Word. Just like the eternal Word, it has a side that speaks to man, and at the same time it remains, like the Word, inwardly veiled in a mystery. And the image strives toward the Word just as man strives toward Christ. Christ and the Word of God are one. He himself said so, with a finite expression that comes forth out of eternity. And the fact that his image-laden Word remains so alive, and is today just as valid as it was then, precisely gives us once again a feeling, a certainty, a sense for eternity.

When, while contemplating, the person praying

looks upon the images of the world in view of the Son—in adoration and love and in the spiritual carrying out of the Creator's will intends them and partakes of them for the Lord—then he also learns in his contemplation how the eternal appears. God does not demand that he become aware of the border that separates time from eternity, but only that he allow himself to be carried over it by the Holy Spirit, whether he is aware of it or not. That he traverse the path between the graspable image and that which is ungraspable, which God lays open to him, between that which he receives through the appearance of the images and the image that once remained veiled to him but is now manifest within the realm of eternal life.

Many things enter into contemplation with a person as points of departure and receive a new meaning in the light of prayer. Other things accompany a person at the same time only at the margins, perhaps simply in order to indicate the passing of time, as a reminder of the whole interconnection of life. Thus, even when she was caught up in ecstatic prayer, Teresa of Avila was not permitted to forget the fish she was supposed to bake. She did not contemplate her activity, nor her own life and tasks. Instead, she contemplated in ecstasy the things of God and was at the same time held bound through the things of her daily life to a reality that is other than the world of ecstasy. Something similar occurs in the usual prayer of contemplation.

God did not create things so that we condemn and forget them, but so that we make use of them, that we place them in the proper light, that we order them in their proper place in our life with God. God desires Teresa's ecstasies, but he also desires that she not lose the measure of earthly things. The highest ecstasy, which can even culminate in the total forgetfulness of self and world, can in a Christian sense never become a contradiction to the most humble work. And the demands that God makes in ecstasy are similar, if not identical, to those that he makes in the most modest work.

The images of things surround prayer like a frame. They form borders and landmarks. And every once in a while they change functions: now they become the image, and contemplation becomes the frame. Between these two there is an exchange and a demand. As long as both are thus interchangeable, work and prayer are genuine, neither one calls the other into question, but both meet precisely at the point of intersection which has been established by God himself for Christian life.

# 9. Images of Heaven

"Whoever sees me sees the Father." With this phrase, the Son opens heaven and grants the believer a glimpse of the eternal vision. The Father lives in the hiddenness of his heaven; no one has seen him except for the Son. But the Son has seen him in such a definitive way that he not merely retains the vision of a Father on earth, but those that believe in him are even able to hear him say, "Whoever sees me sees the Father."

For the disciples, who hear this phrase, it is an astonishing saying: how are they to understand it? Or how can they even begin to try to interpret it? It is as if their belief is not strong enough for it, as if it collapsed before the steep ascent of this vision and could find no foothold in it. They would be prepared to believe the Son that next to him or behind him there was another personal being, the Father, who is distinct and separable from him, just as men are distinct from one another. They would be willing to recognize the Son as a revelation of heaven, and they would even be willing to harbor a hope of being allowed entry into the promised heaven.

But that is not what the Son is saying. The Father and Son are one in being in the Spirit. And so too faith in the incarnate Son and hope for heaven are a single Christian disposition. We see the Son, who lives in our midst, but the life that he lives in our everyday world has its roots in eternity. He has truly entered into history, following a road that allows us to encounter him as often as we wish, a road that we are even allowed to walk with him, because we see and vividly recognize the destination in the Son's journey that was merely intimated in creation. To be sure, we are not able to follow the entire distance that he travels and in the manner in which he walks it, but we are nevertheless able to walk his path. And we have the witness of his apostles and the sacrament of his Eucharist. Wherever he steps forward in a visible way, there the Father too becomes visible in a hiddenness that is nonetheless manifest. And not only the Father, but the Holy Spirit, the eternal Son, the angels and saints and the entire Church of heaven.

The Gospels' words about eternity are spoken in order to familiarize us with the eternal world; what they report is meant just as concretely as the things right before our eyes on earth. "What we have seen, heard, and touched of the word of life", says the Disciple of Love. What he sees he sees in truth. It is a vision of things that he is able to articulate so well in words that they also possess a meaning for us. His descriptions enable us to envision almost the very things that happen in that world, until we come to realize that all of the reports are modified by a "like" and an "as"—that is, the apostle elaborated and translated them in his experience, thereby giving them a super-worldly content. He did not have to equip himself in a special way to receive such visions; they were offered to him. He did not need to coin new, foreign-sounding expressions in order to describe them; what came from heaven presented itself in such a way that it could be translated into earthly terms. What characterizes both levels and orders is that they are governed by the presence of the triune God, the Mother of the Lord, the saints and angels and by the tasks that are meant to be carried out, on the one side, in the apostle's world of heavenly vision, and on the other side, in the earthly world.

The small child asleep in the crib awakens slowly to a knowledge of his mother and his surroundings and finds his place in them. He drinks when the mother offers him her breast; he sleeps when he is laid down to rest. And he makes it known when he is hungry or when his sleep is disturbed, and the mother understands his language. Once he becomes aware, he learns to react in a much more differentiated manner to his surroundings, to recognize and communicate a greater variety of needs; perhaps in the developmental process, new insights, decisions, and capacities have spontaneously emerged. Extending this example, one could characterize the visionary of the apocalypse as one who has become hyper-aware, one to whom suddenly a wholly other knowledge has been given from on high, in order that he might experience the world of heaven and then in turn to return to the earthly world in order to be able to render an intelligible account. He has a perception, and that which he perceives is genuine. And the eyes with which he is able to see were not someone else's; they were his own eyes. And he does not see through foreign glasses, as if his eyes were too weak. The people with whom he speaks are able to see his eyes, which possessed the capacity to see the things of heaven.

And the world that he saw is not merely the Father's world in general, but also the world that is subjected to the Father: the kingdom of God, and the kingdom of evil that is hostile to him. He saw heaven and hell. The essence of both was disclosed through images, irreplaceable images, which the visionary himself does not modify, because they have been prepared for this precise revelation over a long course of time (from the Old Testament). He uses these images in such a way that the listener is able to make the distinction. Moreover, he also sees the decisions made in heaven and the Father's judgment, and he sees these not as mere possibilities, empty threats or promises, but from within their truth, which is made accessible to him. From heaven, he does not separate what the present vision offers to him from what he has learned in the life he has led up to this point; he does not need to leave the one behind in order to take up the other. He lives in a truth that must not be misinterpreted and that does not cease to be something he can grasp. He needs no re-education; God gives to his own what they need and does so not in an extravagance that would surpass the normal human mind, but rather according to simple laws. These laws all belong to heaven, but they nevertheless do not eliminate the laws of the earthly world.

"Today you will be with me in paradise", the Lord promises the thief on the cross. With this word *today*, he overcomes the imminent death in the blink of an eye. Between the thief's hanging on the cross and his being in paradise, the Lord scarcely leaves him the time to die. He builds a bridge into the eternity to come.

Thus the image of heaven stands over the earth, without being separated from the earth by a broad expanse or a temporal distance. What the dying Stephen exclaims is not far from the Lord's utterance on the Cross: "I see the heavens opening!" He sees the gate, the leading of the way, the opening of heaven, and the vision gives him the certainty of having arrived. There will not be any more images to come and eclipse what was now promised; there will be no more delay. The blood witness already crosses the threshold, and what he sees and describes already belongs to the flash of a moment in which the eternal time overtakes the temporal. The Lord provides what the believing heart wishes for and now receives, not in the form of a hope that remains open, but in the certainty of a vision that transcends, an untimely vision that no longer fits into our world. What the thief happens to expect from heaven has now become reality for him through the Lord's words; the Lord releases a whole part of the way; he eliminates the measure of time through his word. Heaven is present. With respect to Stephen's open heaven and the heaven promised on the Cross for today, no more images of heaven are available and conveyed to us; the reality itself takes the place of ephemeral time.

If the Lord speaks to the disciples about the "eternal dwelling-places" or promises them an "eternal banquet" together with him in his Father's kingdom, then these are things of the world, things that once belonged to creation and were entrusted to men for centuries, but henceforward take on the form of a heavenly reality. The Lord's word is truth; and this truth lays hold of the "vine" and the "wine" and transfers them to heaven. This "banquet" will be held in heaven, and the Lord and those that belong to him will be there together. Even for the Lord there is a transcending of time: "No longer now, but afterward." "And you will be with me."

One has to arrange all of the passages together where the Lord speaks of heaven; then these passages can become more pliant. It is difficult to imagine an eternity that preserves our passing days, an infinity, in which there would yet be room for the world's finitude. And yet it is precisely this inconceivable notion that the Lord puts into words. There are many times that he doesn't speak in parables, that he doesn't bracket his words with a "just as" and a "like", but speaks instead with a "that" of certainty and definitiveness. The things spoken with such definitiveness thus belong to faith. This certainty is safeguarded by the Church and has been pondered over for so long that every believer can experience something of it. This experience passes from an earthly, limited and concrete experience over to and into a heavenly one, which is no less concrete.

In this contemplation, objectivity is the first requirement. There may be many things added to this, according to capacity and need, wherein the personal element is also expressed, even to the point of the ebullience of feeling and its outbursts. But this comes only afterward. When the Son of God, whom we worship and who dwells from all eternity with the Father and Holy Spirit in heaven, becomes man and adapts himself to our time and space and human senses, then this happens in the utmost objectivity and appropriateness. We are able to grasp his presence and describe it, just as we are able to describe other things the Father has created. Even more: we are able to observe and contemplate his life. He himself provides us with the matter for such a contemplation, insofar as he offers himself and shows himself to us, insofar as he truly lives in our midst and even finds the way to us in words, words that are adapted to our earthly life and yet are always apt to bring us a glimpse into heaven. This utmost objective appropriateness, which lies in the process of the Incarnation, is therefore not separate from the appropriateness of the eternal triune God in heaven.

In this sense, his arrival forms a counterpart to his promise of the heavenly feast: here, the earthly "vine" and its "yield" suddenly find themselves in heaven, and there, the heavenly Son of the Father suddenly finds himself on earth: in human form, in the time of Pilate, and in the form of Bread and Wine in the time of the Church. In no way do all things thereby become interchangeable; it is not the case, for example, that this chair here would be in heaven, or the heavenly wine would flow on earth.

Nevertheless, there is the possibility of a changing of place (in the seer's vision), and even more: of the simultaneous presence of the seer in heaven and on earth. There is the possibility, in a vision sent by God, to grasp things both in heaven and on earth, in images that stem immediately from heaven and are destined for the earth, for the Church, or for individual believers present in the Church. All of these images of heaven revealed on earth are sent into the Church from heaven, and they thus reflect the fact that the Father, at the world's beginning, created all things in view of the Son. If it is God's will, the images of heaven turn into images that are revealed on earth; he grants them to those who belong to him so that, in their task, they may disseminate living representations of heaven in the Church. And nothing that concerns what heaven is ought to get lost on earth. The presence of the heavenly images on earth has been granted along with the responsibility that these images be preserved.

Thus, we also learn that we have to preserve the things of this world in heaven. They were not created in view of the Son for no reason. Here, too, there is a responsibility, here too the talent must be properly managed. This management belongs to the content of our Christian life; it belongs to the mission of our faith. It never fades away into nothingness but must instead enter into heaven, so that the image that abides on earth may remain useful in heaven, just as the image that has been lent to earth from heaven must preserve its appropriateness.

Both must occur objectively, powerfully, and in accordance with mission. A faith that would lose its images would forfeit its connection with things. Genuine faith speculation is always true and conformed to the reality [*dingfest*], it accompanies a person from one thought-image to the next. It is not the case that a gaping hole stands between the images, swallowing everything up. Instead, this is the point at which the ball that thought bounces touches ground. Here there are moments wherein connections are made and things are gathered up, moments that have of course been established from eternity by providence and that now become visible for the believer who reflects on faith within the Church. The two great reference points that the triune God has granted to our world and our faith are the Son, who fulfilled what was promised in becoming man, and the Church, who is the Lord's Bride from all eternity. Speculation is objective and correct only if it proceeds from the concrete history of salvation and from its fulfillment in Christ and the Church, and only if, in treating these concrete results even in all their abstractions, it always intends and describes the concrete. A person cannot harmonize God's heaven according to subjective images, insights and needs. Once a person has fallen outside of the concreteness of Christian revelation in relation to these, then he will never manage to find his way back. The heaven that forms the object of the Christian's reflection in faith must truly be God's heaven, and the things of this heaven must remain demonstrable, not through mere intellectual games, but through the images of heaven that themselves have been modeled on the images of this earth.

If a person concerns himself with images of heaven in his contemplation, he soon notices how extremely apt they are at enriching prayer. The "I" that will one day become reality in heaven seems so foreign to the "I" that is now contemplating because the future "I" will have once and for all taken its leave from the realm of sin. Whatever is affected by sin will at that point fall away from us like a useless garment, and we will then stand there in a nakedness that is beyond our present capacity to understand. At the same time, everything that has any connection whatsoever with the world of sin will likewise be stripped away from the images.

Until that day, the names used for heaven's images will have a meaning at the earthly level. The image that draws closest to our spirit is that of the Lord, and it does so mostly through his own sayings. But we know that he himself is the Word, and that therefore his sayings will be enough for us all the way into eternity and the infinite. We all have to struggle to keep earthly images and concepts open for this mysterious realm, but God does not allow this effort to be in vain. If we do not whimsically fill up the divine depths of the words of revelation with our own imaginings, but rather open our minds to God in contemplation and present ourselves and offer ourselves to the God who makes himself accessible in revelation, then he will breathe life into our images and fill them with his Holy Spirit.

Earthly things, which we contemplate in relation to the Son, are familiar to us; they have been entrusted to us on earth. But we have not been entrusted with heavenly things; they are veiled in a mystery that to be sure can be known in faith, but that withdraws from our senses. Thus, the contemplation of these things is more spiritual. But it ought not, for that reason, to disappear into a fog, because the Son himself has made the heavenly promises warm and familiar. If we always run the danger in the contemplation of earthly images of becoming fixated on the sensual, then the contemplation of heavenly images forcefully compels us to ascend into the spiritual. It will therefore be best to alternate between both modes of contemplation and to allow each to complement and fructify the other. The immanence of the one must acquire its eternal depth through the other, and at the same time it ought to bring a concrete coloring to the transcendence of the other. Both have their own specificity, but they belong together. Thus, in the course of contemplation, neither one should ever be entirely absent, because the one Word of the Lord always pervades every level: from the level of things graspable by the senses, to that which is most spiritual and beyond our understanding.

There is therefore a contemplation of the incarnate Word as a whole, which must be a thread that runs through all of the contemplations of individual words or aspects. Every contemplation must take its measure from his person, since he is a man among men and at the same time the Father's Word in heaven. Only, the person praying cannot strive to capture the impossible—the mysterious point at which the Word becomes flesh and the flesh becomes bearer of the Word—in a sensuous intuition or a concept. Whoever loves the Son and seeks and adores the Father in the Son will be led to this point in faith.

# 10. The Lord's Parables

Whoever contemplates the miracles that the Lord performs always faces a gap: between the man who dwells among us and the God for whom nothing is impossible. Between what a man can expect and what surprises every expectation. This chasm cannot be overcome through faith, but rather through something ungraspable, through God's immediate intervention, which is something that does not allow itself to be brought into alignment with other things.

Any attempt to illuminate a miracle conceptually, to describe all of its concurrent factors—some more known, some more hidden—will eventually run up against a point that remains beyond the understanding's reach. The human spirit experiences something similar when it contemplates the Son's essence as God made man. As a concrete Person, the Son includes both a human and a divine nature; he thus bridges the chasm that always gapes open between the two for us men. And because the Son is one in being with the Father and because no one has seen the Father except the Son, it is no wonder for the believer that Christ's being remains an absolute mystery, which he can never grasp without repeatedly coming face to face with the inconceivable distance between God and man.

In the parables, this gap is for the most part hidden. The Lord recounts straightforward stories that are wholly intelligible in earthly terms: stories about the "sower", the "fisher's net", the discovered "pearl", and so forth. The words and events have a tangible meaning, so that they can be completely understood in their human meaning by anyone, believer and nonbeliever alike. In the Lord's descriptions, we recognize persons, things and situations familiar to us, things that we have either experienced ourselves or that we can imagine without any difficulty. And yet we nevertheless suddenly find ourselves before the same gap. The account becomes filled with a divine content that calls on the listener's capacity to believe. The infinite word penetrates into the finite, limited word. The sower is no longer just any old farmer; he is the Unique Sower, and the net is the Church, and the pearl is the kingdom of God. The images take this divine meaning into themselves; they do not break down or fall apart, but they nevertheless become transparent to something beyond the world. The old meaning remains something established; it does not need to be torn down in order to make space. It is not so suffused by the radiance of the sunrise that it is totally eclipsed and becomes invisible. On the contrary, through the heavenly meaning, the earthly images acquire a new and wonderful freshness and color: admittedly, not for our aesthetic pleasure, but for the faith that ought to catch sight of something of the essence of heaven through the radiance of color from above.

The parables are at first so straightforward that even children can understand them. In order to draw the attention of children, we ought to speak in the same way and use words like these. But the moment the story's divine meaning becomes visible, then the underlying meaning and the difficulty begin. For the Lord himself who recounts the stories, the entire meaning remains throughout just as clear and childlike, just as obvious and ordinary, as it was at the outset. He therefore does not need to conduct a laborious search to find his examples; he can use what is familiar to him to formulate his images with ease. For us, by contrast, since we are mired in sin and weakness, the heavenly world is unfamiliar, and we must therefore struggle gropingly after it through parables. But we are able to infer from the way in which the parable is told that, here, the one speaking stands above the earthly fog in the clarity of the divine, and in the parable we realize that a divine meaning has been intended for us and granted to us.

Contemplating the parables, we are able to dissect them with our reason; we ask, What is it they seek to articulate? what do they contain? what do they demand? what do they promise and fulfill? But we can also simply allow them to take effect in us as images. In this case, we watch what this sower does and what happens to the seed he scatters. We do so with reverence, aware that this is an image that God has chosen. It is the same reverence that takes hold of us when we pray the Our Father, when we realize that these words were first spoken by the eternal Son and placed in our mouths. In this attitude, it becomes immediately apparent to us that the images in the parables are infinitely worthy of reverence, because the Son found them worthy expressions of the essence of God's kingdom. He takes hold of them, just like a workman takes an object in his hand to test its usefulness, an object that he is able to get much more use out of than any layman would. But what the Lord gets from these images is a divine meaning that no creature would have been able to put into these plain words.

We might perhaps begin to imagine that we ourselves could invent parables like those in the Gospel; they could turn out well, and we would thus flatter ourselves for having created such meaningful stories with God's help. But in no time we would discover that they are nothing but a pale imitation of what the Lord himself said long ago in his own parables; we would realize how much his parables achieve a divine and hidden significance. This meaning does not fade with the passing of time, but instead grows ever more gloriously manifest. Children, to whom one recounts fairy tales, always want to hear them again, in the same order and with the same details; indeed, they interrupt you if you leave something out, and if you change a single detail, they are not happy. The same thing can be said of the parables. Whoever wants to introduce changes—perhaps with the best of intentions, in order to provoke the listener's "religious sense"—would not offer the same thing, but in fact decidedly less. The believer knows that God's word desired to be revealed in a particular form, and not in an undefined way. Precisely *this* form is the bearer of infinite meaning and the springboard for infinite interpretations. The story never comes to an end, and the listener ought never to grow tired of listening to it. Its meaning remains at once clear and inexhaustible, like a spring that never ceases flowing. New meaning constantly streams forth, and new people coming to contemplate can draw refreshment from it, just as the Son's Eucharist is new and unique every day, and offers infinitely more than the one celebrating it is able to take in, even if he daily increases in his capacity to understand and comprehend. Thus, the word means more to the person contemplating every single day, and the image increases daily in its purity and power.

If someone were to require a believer to say something about the kingdom of heaven, he would necessarily resist. Since he does not know the kingdom of heaven from experience, he would have to say

that, though it is the content of his faith and the
goal of his hope, his knowledge does not suffice to
draw a picture of it. The Son alone has the power to
say, "The kingdom of heaven is . . . ," "The kingdom of heaven is like . . . ," and then to call up
some straightforward image from this world. If we
were to take away the beginning of the sentence,
there would be nothing special about what the Lord
says. Everyone has heard or experienced similar stories. It would not occur to anyone that there was
more behind what he said than the everyday meaning. And yet, at the beginning of these stories, the
Lord places the phrase: "The kingdom of heaven
is . . ." Now the earthly parables stand within the
embrace of the infinite and so become the expression of the Father's will, the essence of the heavenly
world. We carry this hidden treasure around with
us in these earthly words and, again and again, we
see something of heaven's glory shine through them
from the treasure chest of the Lord's words, but also
from the normal, everyday experiences these words
relate.

We are all like the little Bernadette, who watches
the spring suddenly burst forth from the earth. A
small child scratches at the soil, but it is a child who
prays, and who, through praying, gains insight. She
does not understand the words that she is supposed
to repeat; she simply utters them mechanically, but
she does so in faith and in the certainty of an encounter. And as the eternal meaning takes hold, the

spring begins to flow. A similar thing happens with the parables about the kingdom of heaven. We deal with them without understanding, and as readers or preachers we are still far from knowing their true sense, the sense that they have in the Son's eyes. But the word becomes radiant, the spring bursts forth, and we experience something of the kingdom of heaven. We have an inkling about it, but one day —no one knows the hour!—it already acquires an eternal value. The meaning of the everlasting kingdom, which will last as long as eternal life, lies in ephemeral words. And as the parable's meaning unfolds, constant points of entry open up into the eternal meaning. The house and the field and the man and the grain and the vine and the fish: they are all no longer something merely from this world, something that passes away and that a person lets go, something that a person is able to ignore: they have become bearers, constitutive parts, of the kingdom of heaven. Indeed, taken as a whole, they contain the kingdom of heaven itself. To be sure, they do not do so in the sense that one can achieve the heavenly whole by adding up the individual images. Nevertheless, every image is an image of the whole, a vessel for the infinite, which can no longer be broken down into pieces.

It therefore follows that the contemplation of individual parables never comes to an end. The person praying must constantly strive to find the treasure hidden in the field. But what is important is not what the person praying reads into the parable, but what already lies within it and which is in fact the kingdom of heaven itself. The word is perfect and complete, and the person praying steadily works his way up to it. What he, as one who prays, has to see and to think and to express in his interaction with the word, may help him to arrive at this fullness and perfection. But the more he discovers, the more certain he also becomes that all of the substance lies in the words themselves, and that others before him and after him, and above all the Lord himself, have seen much more and will see much more in the plain sentence that he contemplates than he: the other believers see a relative "more", the Lord sees the absolute "more" of the undivided eternal meaning.

But it is important to the Lord to portray the kingdom of heaven in such images, because it is important to him that we possess the kingdom of heaven precisely in his words. The Father possesses the Son from the beginning as his Word. But we possess the Father's kingdom in the Son's word, which is itself the word of the Father. Thus, the way to the Father passes through the simple word of the Son. And the Father is not the end and conclusion of this way; rather, he is the beginning. For it is the word of the kingdom of heaven, which, through the Son's word, gives us access to the Father in heaven, the Father of heaven—in images that are so unassuming and ordinary that we believe ourselves too good to ascribe to them a religious meaning. But all of a sudden we are surprised and we marvel, once we see that the Son chose such images—our useless words and empty notions and inadequate concepts, which always come to an end before they can come to complete expression—in order to allow them to become, in his mouth, the kingdom of heaven.

# 11. Images of the Trinity

God the Father himself introduced numbers to man by separating the day from night and by bringing about a particular and unique work in each day of creation. And finally, God made use of number in order to reveal something of his own essence. Not in an exhaustive way, because our concepts of faith come from his revelation alone, and our faith does not belong to us, but to God, in such a way that it is open to God and is constantly nourished by God and can be broadened by him, but it never passes over definitively into our control.

God reveals himself as triune: one being in three Persons. The heart of this mystery remains ever beyond man's grasp. Nevertheless, the Creator created human beings as man and woman, and gave to them both the child; he placed them into a relationship that opens up beyond itself. When a man seeks a woman, he does so from the beginning in the expectation of starting a family. He already loves his children in the woman. But before they arrive, there is first the man and the woman and their hope for the child. They know that their love is permitted to believe in a fullness to come, that love holds a promise in faith. All of this occurs at first in a limited, earthly sense. "Faith" thus rests simply on the experience of other men who have found a wife and had children. And the child was a new beginning, a goal and once again new life and new hope, which points to a new community. This is an image.

The image of the family serves in a sense to bring forth further images. God the Father sent his Son into the world; Mary bore him, Joseph, his foster father, stood by, entrusted with a task that far exceeded his natural capacities, since he, a mere man, was commissioned to represent the almighty, the true Father of the child. An excessive demand was made of his faith from the beginning, and he was taken into a service that he never expected and could not conceive beforehand. Nevertheless, he gave himself to it and carried out what God wanted of him, and he completed his task in a perfect way. He strove to accomplish what was given to him to accomplish, and he was required to give up many things that pleased him. He cleared a space in his everyday life for something impossible to conceive and did not try to figure it out. He lived inside faith, inside a deferential attentiveness. Faith and attentiveness are the sign that a person can be taken into service for a "more" that lies completely in God's hands, in the hands of the Father who sends the Son and of the Spirit who descends upon the mother, and of the Son who lies in her arms as a tiny child. And thus the Trinity acquires a paradigm in the first Christian family, whose center is God himself; it is an image made up of human beings, one of whom was at the same time God and one in being with the heavenly Father. An image that points beyond itself, one that reaches out forward to the Word of the Son and his prayer and learning and his way of the Cross and his death, and that points backward to heaven, whence the grace of redemption came into the world, out of the bosom of the triune God.

These images were genuine events that occurred in the midst of real history. It must not have been easy for Joseph to see God in the little child who was entrusted to him. The defenseless, little creature is the revelation of the eternal Word! The daily growing boy is the human form of the Son who rests from before the creation of the world in the bosom of the Father! The poor, little relationships in Bethlehem or Nazareth are the revelation of eternal life! The neediness of every moment is the image of the almighty God who knows no need! And everything is stretched out and transposed, not dead and disjointed; everything is living and pointing backward and forward and in every direction promising new life and nevertheless always contained within the particular expressed word.

Admittedly, Christ's words constantly transgress boundaries, here into heaven, there into earth; they know no limits. Neither the limitations of space nor the limitations of merely human concepts, nor even those limitations in which man feels so comfortable, which he holds onto in order not to have to accomplish any more, which he re-establishes the moment he fears that they are falling away and that he might therefore lose his protection and stand naked before the eternal God. Even death is removed from its place and changed into a promise and a path. The Son crossed this path and rose again—in such a matter-of-fact way it is as if it were an obvious achievement, as if this crossing were merely the fulfillment of a wholly natural expectation: that the one who was crucified and who died, the one whose death so shook the whole of nature and darkened heaven and broke open the tombs, now still had to rise from the dead and pour out his new life over his disciples, over his mother and the women at the tomb and over the entire Church until the end of time.

Ever since the Incarnation, the Son of God has been present among us in a bodily way. But he is so because the Holy Spirit carried the Father's seed into the Virgin Mother, and thus because the triune God has given himself to us in the Son. We are able to contemplate the child in his mother's womb in no other way than from within his living connection with the Father and the Spirit. To be sure, the fact that we can see the Son in our midst by means of our senses, that we are able to expect from the Child the same things we would expect from a human being, and that we are permitted to watch his growing up and be witnesses to his work, his silence and prayer, and his preaching—all this is an aid to our reflection. But everything that acquires such a sharp profile before our eyes, that acts in such a concrete way, leads us at the same time to what remains hidden in the manifestation, to what is not presented and shown to our senses, to what is spoken in silence. It is the triune mystery in the incarnate Son. A real child stands before us, but he is one in being with the Father and the Spirit. If we attempted to separate his human reality from its connection with the divine, we would falsify the reality, we would make no sense of the boundless and eternal dimension of this human being. We would collapse into a religion of the letter that would empty our faith of all meaning. The Son's Incarnation, which has occurred here, would immediately turn into a contradiction to the triune God's will to Incarnation.

The child is God, and as God he is not bound by our limitations of space and time. He assumed them in order to transform them into gateways to the eternal and unchanging. This transcendence of limitation is not a rejection, but rather a pointing beyond to what is higher. The words the boy spoke in the temple, or the words the man spoke at the wedding of Cana, or later on the Cross, are in their irrevocable character expressions of divine, triune being. He does not point away to something that lies beyond himself; he is not the copy of an original. He is the Son of God himself, who in his concreteness co-presents the concreteness of the Father and the Spirit. And his truth is their truth. And his life is their life.

A number has significance for us in the fact that it distinguishes one thing from the rest and is nevertheless a member of the number series. We would not understand what eleven is if we were unable to see its place between ten and twelve. And the number one would lose all significance if it were not followed by two and three. To be sure, we can remove one number from the series and contemplate it for ourselves and perform operations with it; but doing so presupposes the existence of numbers in general and individual numbers in particular. When we contemplate the Son, we thus constantly presuppose in faith the Father and the Spirit. Even if we are not always aware of them, even if we do not always have before our eyes the relationships between the Son and the other Persons in God. But we must allow the Son to be embedded within these relationships and always try to clarify them for ourselves in images and bring them to consciousness. This is necessary in order for us to keep our faith whole, and also in order for the Church to remain catholic and in order for the Son's entire foundation, with the sacraments, preaching, the interaction with the saints and with the mother of the Lord, to retain its meaning. For this meaning must have its roots in God's triunity, and thereby become inexhaustible, just as everything that the Son reveals of the triune life announces its authenticity through its rooted-ness in the inexhaustible.

If we were to contemplate the Son separately, then his humanity would stand out and we would see him increasingly, and eventually exclusively, as a human being. In this case, the fulfillment would be lacking and the promise would lose its truth, and the whole of revelation would come crashing down. Nothing would be able to be left standing, because the Son would lose any essential connection with the Father who creates and the Spirit who perfects. The dilapidated building that would be left over would no longer offer any opportunity for Christian faith, and soon not even for Old Testament faith. Everything would move merely within the realm of reason, within the realm of the humanly demonstrable. It would essentially have no more meaning than any other human phenomenon.

"Whoever sees me sees the Father." The Son opens our human eyes for eternal vision. He wipes away the boundaries of visibility, in order to include the invisible within the sphere of the visible. And the Word conveys vision in order to lend it the true life of the Spirit. The images of the Trinity are always based on what is graspable by man, who perceives and thinks in terms of the senses, in order, by leaving limitations behind, to convey what lies beyond senses and concepts, by entering into our limitations, the unlimited eliminates them, without destroying them, in order to allow us to participate in the unlimited.

The Son prays the Our Father in the presence of his disciples. He not only invites them into his prayer, but in fact gives them a prayer from his own. It begins by addressing the Father. Then comes heaven, then the earth, bread and the forgiveness of sins. The Church and her sacraments are not only gestured at from a distance, but are embraced in a living way, formed from the Word who is himself the very first prayer. This Word turns to the Father by including not only believers within himself, but also the sacramental bread and the sacramental removal of sin. Thus, the Son, in his conversation with the Father, does not show any reluctance to include in his prayer the earthly things that he brings about—indeed, he himself will become the believers' daily bread and will establish the great absolution of sins on the Cross—just as he requires those around him to pray. They too must therefore speak the word in their manner and make use of the images that he has granted to them. The images of triunity therefore include sacramental images, but they also include heaven and earth, as they ought to be seen by Christians. And the glorification of God and his name. All of the basic concepts that the Son communicated to those who belong to him are thus gathered up together, and all of them join together eternal and temporal life. All of them lie within the Word that the Son both is and expresses.

But they have also all become words of the earth; they have come to us through many generations and we still today discover in them the same living relationship between the Son and the Father, the same trinitarian exchange of love, as the Lord's contemporaries saw. This prayer has overcome time. The words have perhaps undergone a certain shift in understanding that occurs with the passing of the centuries, but they nevertheless have remained unchanged in their essence. Participating in the development of the Church and life in history, they nevertheless point in an infallible way to that which stood at the beginning.

The Our Father, seen as a treasury of images of the triune life, offers the believer a wealth of material, which both constantly opens up things to his understanding and, precisely with this new understanding, also opens new horizons of things that have not yet been understood. And this material does not appear to the believer with the hardness of an unmoveable boulder, but rather like the undulating sea of God's ever-greater love. Love remains something both offered and demanded. But the whole is the world of discipleship: that of the Son, who follows after the Father, and that of the disciples, who follow after the Son. And thus the images, which the Son himself fashions and designs, which he as God disposes [*anordnet*], arranges [*einordnet*], and coordinates [*zuordnet*] as he sees fit, are images drawn from eternal life, which reveal triune love. We receive a certain sense for their provenance when we discover that this prayer has lost nothing of its power and life with the passing of centuries, and thereby gives us an intimation of what it means to stand before the face of the eternal God and praise him eternally.

God created man in his own image. Men thus learned—and they have always known something of this—they have come to understand, that they have to display something that lies in God. It thus follows that, in everything they possess and are as human beings, in everything that happens to them, presents and offers itself to them, in everything they know and study, in whatever they are capable of acquiring, they must take heed of the image; they must look upon the image that they themselves are. This does not mean they must contemplate themselves, because self-contemplation is something that quickly comes to an end once man becomes aware of the greatness of God. But rather the image that they themselves are, because by looking upon God's greatness, they become transformed into this image that God intended. Thus, by creating man in his image, God created a creature that *becomes* capable of contemplation; a creature that, because he is an image, must keep his eyes on the original, and because he has been created, must turn his face toward the Creator.

At the same time, God gave him a countless number of images in the cosmos, of which man has gained ever deeper knowledge. Some are completely recognizable, just as a stone on the side of the road is recognizable and can be grasped in one's hand, but some are more mysterious, like a plant that unfolds itself out of the dark seed buried in the earth until it brings forth a blossom and fruit. The greatest mysteries, which are mysteries of God, arch over all of these like a vault. And insofar as these concern images for trinitarian life, it is perhaps man's most beautiful task to be permitted to contemplate these, to approach them with open eyes, in order to draw close to God by means of his senses, his striving, and his contemplation, not along lonely and esoteric paths, but along the very path that the Son himself walked.

In this way, whatever is ephemeral in man, and

whatever is ephemeral in the temporality to which he is bound, is reflected back into the eternal, is brought into a circularity, which is not the circle of the world that passes away, not the circle of the stars and the ages of the world, but is the circle formed by the Son in his coming from and returning to the Father, a movement that reveals the eternal circle of trinitarian love.

All of the signs and signifiers for the Trinity, which lie within Scripture and which the Church's tradition has unfolded, and the Church's entire treasury of prayer, in which the thoughts and insights and discoveries of countless praying people are preserved and stored in a fruitful way, are included in this return. They lie within this return just as the whole of salvation history is recapitulated in the Son: all of the prophets' voices and all of the apostles' self-surrender and the surrender of those who have come after them, and all things together, converge in the contemplation that the Son established together with his brothers in Spirit and in Truth.

Thus, contemplation shows itself to be the inevitable and sole necessary way to let the Father's will be done on earth in a fruitful way, and to be so devoted to heaven that God's revelation in the Word remain ever living and relevant. To be sure, revelation came to an end with the apostles, but it remains true in another sense that revelation begins anew every single day. Revelation will remain at the beginning for as long as the world endures: for the word that the Son spoke and enacted once and for all is able to reveal in ever greater depth the things of the infinite God.